Ray O. McElain

D1214414

IF WITH
ALL YOUR
HEART

Roy O. McClain

Fleming H. Revell Company

IF WITH

ALL YOUR

HEART

Dedication

To Atlanta's First Baptist Church—that household of faith whose unstinting love and unmeasured generosity have created a spiritual climate in which religious duty becomes daily delight. . . .

To multi-hundreds in that congregation whose voluntary loyalties have challenged the best within me. . . .

To a good staff whose qualitative team spirit has made possible achievements in this ministry for which I have received credit. . . .

To the leaders in this family of God who daily evaluate time and circumstance in order to give priority to God's Kingdom. . . .

I affectionately dedicate this book—with all my heart.

Foreword

MODERN MAN STANDS gripped in a self-consciousness of his newly found powers and their distracting responsibilities. A halting, wavering confusion is much in evidence today. A dismaying world is taking shape before our eyes: a world of automation and the depersonalized man; of Sputnik, Honest John, and solar prophets; a world with a new idiom. Being neither patient with the old structures nor courageously enthusiastic about the new ones, today's citizen possesses an uncertainty and insecurity without parallel. As a result, anxiety has intensified the uncertainty. Gnawing guilt lies heavily upon modern man as he plans excursions to outer space, guilt resulting from the mediocre quality of his citizenship on this planet which he knows is a poor recommendation for inhabiting other planets.

Every second another child is born in our world. Fifty million each year! The environment in which many are born is devoid of every semblance of God, freedom, human decency or purposeful living. One-third of the human race and one-fourth of the world's area are under the domination of pagans who belligerently shout: "There is no God!" This infamous line, whether it flows from Marxist presses or from lips of next-door neighbors, is the crucial testimony of unbelieving masses. Apocalyptic prophets with their neurotic contemplations of mass destruction are adding their disconsoling voices to a long filibuster of doom and predictions of mega-death.

Whereas once an inviting voice said, "Come over to Macedonia and help us," that voice has changed its message. Few are beckoning to the free world nowadays to come over and help. Instead, the message is reversed: "Don't come over to Macedonia, because we don't want your help." Or, "Since you were so long coming we decided that Troas was more important to you; anyway, others have come to help—others who have pledged themselves 'to bury you.' "

In such disquieting times, it is not enough to diagnose world conditions. Demonstrating a cure is the only effective method that will have worthwhile results.

A PROFILE OF DEPERSONALIZED MAN

The currents of popular opinion are running against the ideal of personality. Mass movements, herd thinking, and group actions are depersonalizing the individual to the extent that he becomes a mere unit of production. Under this absorbing sponge, the person not only has diminished concern about himself, but has developed an apathetic outlook which makes him susceptible to every whim of doctrine, as well as easy prey to self-appointed authorities who would exploit him. Today's man, like a rubber ball having lost its elasticity, rolls with the slightest push. Being true to one's inner nature, trying to harmonize deed with character becomes harder every day. Upon surrendering his personal identity to the herd, he surrenders also his personal, moral judgment. The ill results are much like a civil war within. Endorsing what the masses say is good and condemning what they say is evil, he often must ride roughshod over his own convictions until they are shunted to one side where they lie ignored and eventually forgotten. Stripped of his own soul, the depersonalized man rationalizes such servile nakedness by depending on a parasitic attitude: i.e., Uncle Sam will take care of us; or, the government will look after our interest, or at least the welfare department.

Pursuing his group-determined direction, still he isn't sure of his route or his destiny. Lacking mental collectedness, he easily is lost in a maze of contradictory voices. Right at this point the dispensers of collectivism and mass determinism must be called into account. They are creating a society wherein some men are merely raw material in human form for other men. In the name of truth and reason there is an endless parade of insulting invective, nauseating cruelty, belligerence decently veiled, and vulgar provincialism masquerading as patriotism. These are the ugly faces of soulless men,

8

who somewhere along the line had all the corners of their personalities rounded out by abrasive conformists. Byron's uncharitable quip about a former era is timely remembered in this generation:

> Society is now one polish'd horde,
> Formed of two mighty tribes, the *Bores* and the *Bored*.[1]

OUR RELIGIOUS DILEMMA

A tame, religious sterility to which we have become accustomed now must face its modern accusers. Faith that was to have removed mountains is having difficulty moving molehills, not because it is powerless, rather, because puny, partial deployment hasn't given faith a chance to reveal its dynamic properties. Preoccupation about religious living, about being good, at the expense of loving and obeying God has led to a type of ecclesiastical egomania which expresses itself in petty policies, religious trivia and "little churchinesses." Foreign to the New Testament pattern, this lack of inwardness is reflected in a thousand-and-one facets of activistic religion. Setting goals of being good as though vital Christianity would occupy its time with such self-concern is waste of effort. Such moral perfectionism ignores the Biblical fact that being "perfect" in the eyes of Jesus means being "usable."

Militant Christianity is beating a retreat into the safe precincts of organized religion. Fearing most things controversial, retreating religion prefers playing it safely. But genuine religion, like real music, needs no defensive strategy. Good music needs to be played—not defended. Just so with Christianity: the crutches designed to support it are unnecessary for the simple reason that vital faith does not limp.

The impasse of contemporary religion is the result of the efforts of unreconstructed men to reconstruct society. Believing that weak men can build an enduring, strong world is folly of the first magnitude. Such contention is not new, but today it has a host of new exponents. The "do-it-yourself-in-six-easy-lessons" plan of salvation is regular fare in many churches. With success guaranteed, these

[1] Lord Byron, "Don Juan," Canto XIII, Stanza 95.

9

happy-thought apostles leave the impression that all life's problems are within easy solution if only one becomes familiar with certain jargon, easy rote and shallow "togetherness." Naturally this sugar-coated brand of religion attracts millions who want instant religion, much as they want instant coffee, which requires no disciplines of time or sacrifice. Learn the magic words and prayer becomes a sort of automation in which a prayer down, and a prayer a day is a better way to get what you want than a charge-a-plate! In the mouths of happy-talk preachers, faith is a panacea assuring sound health, material prosperity and longevity to all who embrace it. A diet of pablum indeed! No wonder there is so little muscle in our moral fibre. This pre-digested, sentimental religion does not remotely resemble New Testament Christianity. Making a cross central in redemption, a strait gate the exclusive entrance, and a narrow path the singular route to life eternal, Jesus Christ scoffed at easy religion while joyously proclaiming that the steep ascent to heaven still is through "peril, toil and pain."

When future historians have written their commentaries on our way of life, in all probability they will attribute our lack of effectiveness to halfhearted religion. Failing to take God seriously, major emphasis is on making a living, often at the expense of making a life. And while there have been individuals in every decade who have yielded to God in full-hearted devotion, these have constituted only a tiny minority of the human race. The rank and file of humanity has never known a personalized dedication to holy things. To these throngs, religion has been a sort of necessary evil, uncommitted, designed as a stricture in which custom and conduct are held together. Unfortunately, this concept has changed little in the twentieth century. A vital Christianity speaking of soul-revolution, of about-face and a new birth, strikes them either as superstition or as emotional weakness. Regarding religion as a passive thing to fondle and protect instead of a force to be let loose in their lives, they slam the door on religion when it would speak about politics, race relations, education and personal morality. Some sincerely believe that Christianity should not say a single word about any controversial subject. It is this fearful ignorance that is endangering our rightful place of leadership in the world community. The height of absurdity is reached when one thinks that an impotent, tame faith is sufficient for this cynical, demanding generation. If Nero fiddled while Rome burned, at most his fiddling was a tragedy of errors in one act. But the fiddling of the free nations today is a multi-act tragedy in that the whole world is a tinderbox, with arsonists fanatically eager to ignite it.

The Book of Ecclesiastes records a verse which aptly depicts present-day religion: "Be not righteous over much. . . . Be not over much wicked." This cautious advice suits the average religious conformists who want just enough religion to be respectable but not enough to be devout. Little wonder there is such leanness of soul, such spiritual anemia. The frantic concern about personal happiness ignores the fact that happiness is a by-product of another activity: selfless devotion to something and Someone bigger than ourselves. We lack that inner citadel of soul-serenity, not so much because it is difficult to obtain, but because, ignoring its importance, our quest of it calls for so little heroic sacrifice. Thus impoverished, the mesmerized life plods on its dreary journey.

The ulcers which belong to pagan worrying, sores belonging to hands that have toiled at sin, battlefields caused by a world at cross-purposes with God, partitions which divide church and society— all these easily can be traced to man's partially invested heart and soul.

The halfhearted are apt to spend their best years in frantic quest of material things. Obsessed by a mania for more things, such compulsion wears and tears at life until it sours, loses its lustre, and comes to an end of regret and disappointment. Lacking the glad glow which belongs to one who is annexed to noble deeds and wholehearted devotion, this type of person, when confronted with ill-fortune, is proned to shrivel and sink into despair and defeat. Then halfway cleverness tries to compensate for having missed the main reason for living—that moment of truth which spells the difference between existence and marking time. Of all the worthless people in the world, the most worthless is the man who has missed the purpose for which life is intended. Said one of the biographers

11

of Napoleon, "He was an embarrassment to God." Why? Because Napoleon, like his modern counterparts, did not place his life alongside that divine pattern. Such arrogant refusal is at once both a curse to humanity and an embarrassment to God.

IF WITH ALL YOUR HEART . . .

The purpose of this book is to attempt the completion of the above "if" clause. What happens in life if one's whole heart is invested? If with all your heart you work, live, pray, lift, play, dream and wonder . . . what are the results? Unimaginable! Superlatively unlimited! Life will expand at every seam, giving new dimension to the whole affair. When one willingly deposits his total heart in God's central purpose, then all other pleasures and pursuits pale into relative insignificance.

Jesus promised this type of abundant living. Full-bodied, overflowing, unrationed plenty is afforded to those risking souls who, unafraid to enjoy the stress of abundant living, do not presume that such is possible without all the heart's investment. Religion, under such conditions, is a delight. A catalyst is given to what otherwise would be considered dull duty. The initiative of life is like touching a thistle: touch it timidly and the thistle pricks the hand. Seize the thistle boldly and its spine will crumble in your hand. Courage to seize life with firm grip is a prime need today. The biggest room in our world is the room for improvement.

> Unless above himself he can
> Erect himself, how poor a thing is man![2]

It all adds up to an urgent admission that Christian faith has something to say to this day and generation. Impoverishing this life in favor of life to come is neither the message of Jesus nor the need of the hour. " 'Tis heaven below my Redeemer to know." Our goal is not a stagnant sterility of "peace of mind"—but rather the art of living zestfully, unapologetically, with an enthusiasm which does not deny anxiety but conquers it. Faith that accepts apprehensive

[2] Samuel Daniel, "To the Countess of Cumberland," Stanza 12.

12

doubts without ceasing to enjoy life is the same faith which knows that if one falls out of God's right hand, he will be caught in God's left hand. Remembering that God never closes a door without raising a window, the man of faith knows that though God will bend, He will never break. Sometimes God's best opportunity is at the point of man's direst extremity. And underneath it all are His everlasting arms.

And having thus chosen our course with pure purpose and undiluted love, let us renew our faith in God and go forward without fear and with all our hearts.

Contents

CONTENTS

Introduction

IN 1933 in his book *Modern Man in Search of a Soul,* Carl Gustav Jung wrote:

Among all my patients in the second half of life—that is to say, over thirty-five—there has not been one whose problem in the last resort was not that of finding a religious outlook on life. It is safe to say that every one of them fell ill because he has lost that which the living religions of every age have given to their followers, and none of them has been really healed who did not regain his religious outlook. This of course has nothing whatever to do with a particular creed or membership of a church.

Here, then, the clergyman stands before a vast horizon. But it would seem as if no one had noticed it. It also looks as though the Protestant clergyman of today was insufficiently equipped to cope with the urgent psychic needs of our age. It is indeed high time for the clergyman and the psychotherapist to join forces to meet this great spiritual task.

The great psychiatrist saw with prophetic insight almost thirty years ago that Christianity and psychotherapy have a common meeting ground and could be allies. He almost predicted what has come to pass when he said, "It is indeed high time for the clergyman and the psychotherapist to join forces to meet this great spiritual task."

Since Jung wrote there has been a remarkable development along the lines he visualized. The pastor today who does not do some counseling is beginning to be the exception. A flood of books on pastoral care and counseling continues to issue from the presses of numerous publishers. Courses in pastoral care are the accepted thing in American seminaries and divinity schools. The remarkable development in this field is highlighted by the pioneering work of men like Richard K. Young at Winston-Salem, North Carolina, and in Southeastern Baptist Theological Seminary at Wake Forest. In-

17

deed, we might describe the line of progress as "from Jung to Young."

In this recent development in the field of pastoral care we see evidence of the church's rediscovery of the individual and of the true existential nature of the gospel. Here is a new practical application of the old gospel truth that man in his sin is caught in the complexities of his existence and must be purged of his sin (and sins) in order to find his authentic self. That truth had been for too long submerged in formal religion and a static view of salvation that failed to deal effectively with the root of his trouble, his estrangement from God, his fellows and his real self.

We are witnessing today this problem of man's estrangement approached not only from the alliance between Christianity and psychotherapy, but also from the standpoint of an existential emphasis in theology. Here again we should emphasize the fact that the gospel has always been "existential" in the real meaning of that term. We might say that Paul was the first "existentialist" theologian. What but true existentialism is: "I have been crucified with Christ, and no longer I live but Christ lives in me"? What but existentialism is his description of the great inner struggle of the individual under law described in the seventh chapter of Romans?

So we may affirm that the rediscovery of the individual in his existential situation in both the alliance between Christianity and psychotherapy, and theology, is great gain. But a word of caution is in order. Psychotherapy and pastoral care can never be substituted for Christian experience and both must be thoroughly grounded in the Bible and the gospel in order to be arms of the Christian faith. Furthermore, existentialism in theology must stick close to the Bible lest it become more philosophy than theology. As a philosophy with un-Biblical presuppositions it may well become a resurgence of ancient gnosticism with its heretical docetic and Cerenthian expressions.

It is encouraging to know that a number of the younger preachers of our day are alert to the new theological and religious movements and that they are struggling to find expression of these in their preaching and in their pastoral ministry. It is also reassuring to ob-

18

serve that among them are many who, while accepting the help of the new tides of thought, refuse to be carried into extremes that would do violence to the gospel. Such a preacher is Dr. Roy O. McClain, pastor of the First Baptist Church of Atlanta. In the pages of this, his second book, Dr. McClain reflects the influences of the new movements but at the same time demonstrates his fidelity to the Bible and the gospel. He reveals his awareness of the world we live in and his struggle to relate the gospel to the problems and challenges of our time. It is evident that Dr. McClain, while alive to the seething social issues that confront him and his great church in the metropolis of the South, has not lost sight of the individual in the crowd. Popular as a preacher, in demand as a speaker in many places, administrator of a great city church, Dr. McClain writes as one who believes that a preacher should fulfill the office of prophet, speaking to the people the word of God in a grand and awful time.

For me it is a privilege to write these words of introduction. Dr. McClain was my student and has been my dear friend for a number of years. At Southern Baptist Theological Seminary in Louisville he was my teaching fellow. Since those days I have trusted him and have followed his progress with joy.

EDWARD A. McDOWELL
Southeastern Baptist Theological Seminary,
Wake Forest, N. C.

IF WITH
ALL YOUR
HEART

Creative Tension

1

The same heat that causes a cut flower to wilt, causes a rooted flower to grow.

"I am pressed by two straits . . ."
—*The Apostle Paul.*

A CONCERT OF voices heard on every hand is saying, "Take it easy," "Slow down," "Time out to live," "You're killing yourself at fast pace." Moreover, it describes the perfect state of living as having enough money to retire on a small farm, to be free from nagging necessities, endless schedules, deadlines, and bumper-to-bumper traffic. This advice, heard from pulpits, editorials, best-selling books, radio commentators and street-corner prophets, while sounding convincing, largely is untrue. The impression is being made that if life could be robbed of its tensions, all would be well.

Mere mention of the word "tension" alerts fears ranging from coronaries to clinical psychiatrists. Ulcers, nervous breakdowns, cancer—all these parade through the mind like galloping ghosts at the slightest sign of tightening up. A stampede to drugstores last year resulted in the sale of nearly a quarter of a billion dollars' worth of tranquilizing drugs.

The story not being told in this connection is that much of this fear has no basis in fact. The thing most feared is a definite asset: normal, creative tension is one of man's best possessions. The power of tension to kill has been exaggerated. Without a certain amount of creative tension, life would be flat and inert. Normal tensions power the human machine for peak performance. Take all the tension out of a spring on a door and the door sags on its hinges; too much tension, of course, causes it to slam in your face. Fortunately, the choice is not limited to these extremes.

23

Misunderstanding the nature and role of creative tension, a generation has grown up in the Christian Church with an aversion to this kind of tension. It is this misunderstanding which accounts in part for a spectator attitude toward Kingdom things, a passive, "let-the-other-fellow-do-it" inclination. Such a tendency regards forthrightness as haste, zeal as overdoing the job, nominal concern as potential fanaticism, and achievement as the result of perfectionist slave-driving. Theirs is the ideal of a millennium where the verbs "to go," "to tell," "to witness," "to move," are nonexistent. To have everything under control, to permit no controversial issue on the agenda, and to hear the consoling words of sweetness and light is the zenith of desire among this deceived generation.

It is folly enough to place prime values on activistic religion, but it is worse to compound such folly by setting no action as an ideal. This is the generation that has written its own interpretation of the great commission which Jesus gave to His disciples. Their "revised" version says, "Go ye into all the world and relax, take it easy, and fit in." That Old Testament passage is a favorite for the group: "Speak soothingly to my people. . . ."

What disconcerting contrast to this reasoning are the rebuking words of Jesus in His parable of the rich fool. "Soul . . . take thine ease. . . ." Then Jesus counters, "Thou fool, this night thy soul shall be required of thee. . . ." "Woe to them that are at ease in Zion . . ." still rings a prophetic warning. In our world when millions are aligning themselves against God, this type of tensionless religion is as justified as giving a sleeping pill to a race horse just before the race.

THE NATURE AND ROLE OF DESTRUCTIVE TENSION

There is a type of tension which is as lethal as poison. To isolate it and familiarize ourselves with its nature is not fear but intelligent faith. Pathological tension is a mental and physical state in which life is diverted from the main course and made to travel over rocky roads. The mind knots to such an extent that rational thinking is nearly impossible. The physical body displays a legion of symptoms that are mostly functional in nature. Yet, to the tensive sufferer gripped by such a hold, the pain is real nonetheless. Fortunately, this type of tension is relatively rare. Any condition approaching pathological tension should be avoided. Life cannot be a fruitful, enriching experience so long as negative downdrafts of cutting stress pull at life night and day.

THE MAGNITUDE AND SCOPE OF DESTRUCTIVE TENSION

"But you see Doc, it's like this: my work absorbs me, I can't sleep at night, and I am living on the ragged edge of my nerves." In similar vein the nervous man poured out his familiar story to the British physician. When he had finished reciting the long list of pains and problems, the doctor advised, "Why don't you take off a few days and have a complete change of scenery and action? Go to the circus and see the great Grimaldi—that wonderful clown who will make you laugh and forget your troubles; perhaps then you would return to your work and old routine a new man." The complaining, embarrassed patient answered, "But you see, Doctor, I am Grimaldi!"

No age group seems to be immune from the destroying powers of negative tension. Year-old babies through teen-agers are numbered among ulcer sufferers as well as middle-aged and elderly men and women. It is almost impossible to measure the extent of this modern malady. For a number of years I have kept records on the number of funerals conducted. The files show that more men are buried in the decade between forty-five and fifty-five years of age than between fifty-five and seventy. Of course, these are the stair-climbers, the status seekers, the would-be executive type with whom business competition and the mania for more are ever prevalent.

In the human makeup, one central registry of pathological tension is the coronary region. During the span of years covered by World War II, a third of a million men were killed in combat or died as a result of war. During the same period in America, two million men died from heart failures—many of these the direct result of mounting tensions.

Hypertension is as familiar to our way of life as the morning newspaper. This monolithic impostor has become a permanent guest in modern personalities. Duodenal ulcers and their peptic cousins—the "badge" of the successful executive—stem from functional activities interlaced and interrelated with hypertension. A profile of this type of person is monotonously familiar: a proverbial fingernail eater, a walking civil war with a built-in nervous breakdown. He goes from clinic to clinic, church to church, "faith" healer to "faith" healer, prescription counter to prescription counter, with the variety of would-be cures merely aggravating the nature of the condition.

Honesty forces a near-contradictory admission that many ministers are not exempt from the same sort of life-destroying tensions: trying to ride the escalator of grief and joy, entering the climate of grief with the dying in one hour and then, with the agility of a hydromatic emotional gearshift, changing to the environment of levity with the marrying while running the whole gamut of emotional overtones in between. With little time to let the emotions simmer down, accumulative hypertension, even in the most devout personality, takes a devastating toll.

It is easy to rationalize, "I had rather burn out than rust out," thus placing too great limits on the alternatives. Fortunately, an intelligent sense of values indicates that neither course is necessary: rust nor fire! There are times and occasions requiring fervor and zeal as intense as white heat; but other circumstances demand inactivity, which is essential to resuscitation and repair. A stewardship of responsibility includes the nervous systems as well as material possessions. Few remember that the question, "Know ye not the body is the temple of the soul?" is still in the Bible. We are promised three score years and ten but, if care is not exercised, there is no guarantee that seventy years will be the score. A good guarantee that life will be cut short is to fill it with lethal tension.

There are endless forces that trigger the tensive state of things. Temper, when allowed full force, can recoil in ugly rancor extracting compound taxes from the human spirit. Tears that flow from lost tempers add their liquid liabilities to the stress. Once again, the choice is not between controlling the temper to the point of stuffing resentment and hate in the subconscious cellars of the soul, or flying off the handle at the slightest provocation. Paul, the Apostle, admonished the Ephesians: "Be ye angry and sin not." This advice is not the contradiction in terms which it appears to be. Anger that has no kin in belligerency, indignation that is incensed by vulgar travesty on truth are assets. But let no comfort come from the belief that a child of God can explode with a bad-spirited temper and still be an exemplar of the Christlike spirit. Not so! The very same verse warns that the sun should not go down on one's wrath. Many a midnight of tormenting tension could be obviated by practicing the simple art of reconciliation and forgiveness before going to bed. To expel the evil feelings from the heart before the day is done is a wholesome imperative. We should not encourage the devil by "nursing our wrath to keep it warm." Indignation that has a basis in justification can be given direction by mature, Christian faith. To make anger a righteous virtue, let it be sustained until the causative evil which made it possible is disposed of once and for all.

Many lives are filled with hypertension by the failure to guard the vines from the little foxes which destroy the tender grapes. Most of our lives are not made of big events. As a matter of fact, there are few big moments in any of our lives. Our months and years are but totals of little events, tiny decisions, minute choices, and petty points, and it is in these areas where tensions mount. A few grains of grit in one's shoe can destroy the joy of taking a walk through lovely woods. An annoying speck in one's eye can blur the joy of seeing. A small particle in the delicate mechanism of a ship's compass can throw the needle off course. Just so in human personality. If life's little forces are not controlled, there is small use in trying to control the major ones. A word unfitly spoken, a sarcastic sneer, a vote for the wrong objective, attendance at the wrong place, little deeds of kindness and joy left undone have a way of adding their minus signs to life's stresses. Conversely, the positive counterparts of these stresses work just as effectively in the right direction.

27

Memory is a bank of assets: a lingering handclasp, a potted plant received on a dark, dingy day, two short paragraphs enclosed in a personal letter that become verbal muscles of encouragement when needed most, a pat on the back by the one whose endorsement was so essential when a job was done well—there are practical, inexpensive therapies which can counteract more frustrating tensions than can all drugstores combined.

A microscopic focus on life triggers more than its share of lethal tensions. Some things simply can't be seen in rightful perspective without looking far into the distance. The immediate outlook may be nothing more than a maze of confusion. Who can predict the course of events for half a decade? No one dares venture an informed guess as to the nature and pace of life a decade from now. Still, if God is in the driver's seat, then to ask where God is going during the next decade is the question of first importance.

MISPLACED SENSE OF VALUES— SOURCE OF TENSION

An interminable rat-race in which most of us must live shows few signs of slackening its pace or reducing its toll in human casualties. Yet, there is an answer. It is not in finding more free time or in throttling the speed of society's gears, but in an intelligent sense of values which gladly admits that most things which drive and aggravate do not really matter—either in the short run or the long. To permit a sense of values that would whittle every issue down to the same common denominator is absurd.

This is the paradox of current living. Settling for secondary values, the desire for primary ones lessens day by day. Out on a spur-line detour from important involvements, modern man contents himself in absorption with plastic blocks, laminated panels and barbecue spits. And all this trivia while the world seethes and surges in social upheaval!

For instance: Americans spend more for chewing gum than they do for educational scholarships; more for greeting cards than for medical research! What a degraded sense of values—like putting a ninety-eight-cent price tag on a ten karat diamond while placing a ten-thousand-dollar price tag on costume jewelry. This "tail-wag-ging-the-dog" outlook sets in sharp focus a comedy of errors and at the same time a misdirection. The personal victim of this im-balance retains enough sensitivity to experience a twinge of guilt in the process, but not enough to lead on to contrition and change. Hence, the cross fire of emotional frustration which grows with repetition of effort.

THE EFFECTS OF NEGATIVE TENSION

Let there be no mistake about it: pathological tension will kill you! All the exhortations to roseate thinking notwithstanding, this type of stress is as deadly as a serpent's venom. Looking at its lethal effects may help prevent such devastation in your own life or others.

When life gets in the grip of negative tension, every minor situ-ation mobilizes the forces within the human body as though a major battle were to be fought. Involuntary muscles constrict, causing a general tightening up all over the voluntary system. Blood pressure skyrockets while normal digestive processes are thrown out of bal-ance. Following this alarm mechanism, hot flashes register on every screen of the personality's make-up. Then the citadel of sense—the brain—becomes impaired momentarily, causing old forces of worry, anxiety and fear to act in destructive concert. Under these storm-like circumstances, ofttimes judgment is reduced to the vanishing point.

Unfortunately, this type of tension is not self-limiting. Instead of cooling off once the crisis has passed or the issue settled, it remains at fevered pitch. Then, like a motor that has no cut-off switch, the whole body wears and tears the nervous system unnecessarily. Night and day the whine and whirl of the human motor continues. That such activism is a destroyer of life's best assets—security of emo-tional balance, joy, and relaxed living—goes without saying.

Contrary to a common notion that one works better under this type of tension, the very opposite is true. No great works of art were done by men out of breath, though normal tension that came in the

29

homestretch of creative accomplishments was an asset—but not the type which paralyzes the creative faculties of mind and spirit.

In old Damascus, that most ancient of cities, bead making is a lively art. Rare shades of amber are delicately blended to give the beads their distinctive quality. Standing before these time-honored artisans one is amazed by their paced cadence. The bead maker will stop at regular intervals as though he had lost interest in his work. Experience has taught him that the amber beads will fly apart if handled too often. Electricity generated from friction of frequent handling causes the beads to burst into many pieces. The pace, the cadence is a modern parable. The beads of our emotional composition fly apart from frictional frequencies too. Just being still at regular intervals could be saving therapy for millions who are haunted by fears of failure, hounded by a goal to break last week's quota, prodded by the boss's insistence that "we must make the best better." The mystery is not that so many fly apart in such conditions, but that more do not.

THE NATURE AND ACTIVITY OF CREATIVE TENSION

When proper credence has been placed in the destructive activities of pathological tension, then we are in position to look at the opposite type of tension and its equally opposite effects. No assets of human nature outrank the drive-shaft of life. I have chosen this term to denote the keyed force in life which propels the human machine upward and onward. The finest airplane is still an earth-bound vehicle until it gains necessary altitude required for flying. Racing the motors while taxiing up and down the runways is essential for the take-off; but it is only when the pilot pulls that "stick" back that the nose of the plane tilts upward. Just so in the ascending thrusts of life. Many seem equipped for the journey: theirs are all the accustomed appointments and faculties. There is plenty of sound and good intention. Yet the fact remains that many people never go anywhere in particular, except up and down the runways—or around in circles.

30

One may call it a delicately balanced metabolic pattern, built-in drive, nervous energy, glandular output, perfectionist power, obsessive compulsion or what he will. I call it the life-force, divinely imbedded in human make-up; not an indiscriminate capacity, but a divine endowment by which an individual is to accomplish God's will on earth. In this analytical sense, then, self-regulating tension intensified by periodic acceleration can be one's primal asset. When such a sense of balance exists, then mind, body and soul become a concert of positive harmony. Much like the fireman and engineer of the old-fashioned steam engine, who, knowing that a steep incline was near, fired the boiler to maximum pressure, opened throttles to command the iron giant's full force, causing air, carbon, smoke, moisture and gases to whirl in tornadic fury, creating strength for steel arms to turn the laboring wheels.

In the human locomotive, the person looks out at the steep hill of decision. Sometimes this consists of mountains of work to be done, or inclines of financial challenge. Maybe grief's rocky road is straight up. When faced with climbing, constructive tension, like the fireman's boiler, begins to build up by conscious effort. A slight rise in blood pressure and pulse occurs. A command to tighten up goes out from the brain to the lungs and heart. Stomach muscles tense in firm reaction, causing the large voluntary muscles of arms, legs and body to respond like the instruments of a symphony. In the citadel of the brain, the senses become perceptibly sharpened: memory, judgment and quick thinking are set in sharp focus. Controlled anxiety surrounds the personality.

Then, once the crisis is passed, the hill climbed, the problem solved, the slack-off begins. This is comparable to the situation of the fireman aboard his locomotive: when no more coal is thrown in the boiler for a while, the iron soldiers hear "At ease." The human nervous system, informed by the brain that the occasion for keying up has passed, sets its soldiers at ease. So, the simmer down, the shutting off of steam causes tension to subside, just as normally and inevitably as the tide returns to its deeper cradle after washing the sands of the beach. Herein is the safety valve, the built-in, self-limiting nature of positive tension. So long as the brain

31

makes it clear to the muscles that adrenalin and sugar enough for each hard pull are stored in their bins, the body will be able to measure up to most of the demands made on it.

Without the ability to work up crisis-ready tension, no oration would be delivered with inspirational fervor, no steady strokes would be sent in the direction of creativity. Nor would caution, in the face of danger, be timed right. It is the lightning flash of positive fear at the brink of disaster that causes the right foot to apply the brakes. So, here is a qualitative aspect of our nature that should activate prayers of gratitude rather than a rush to the drugstore for chemicals to stifle the capacity.

PERSONAL SUCCESS AND THE ROLE OF SOUL-STRESS

It is with weighted reluctance that I mention the word "success." What thin, acrid content shows in many contemporary "successful" men and women. But if, for our purpose here, we agree that despite the illusive nature of success, one who sets himself to a noble task, whose motives extend beyond his own ego, performs that task expeditiously, then to some extent he has succeeded.

Be that as it may, one fact is indisputably clear: no great works of art are created by the even-tempered, always-agreeable soul who shrinks from all tension. The biographies of renowned sculptors, musicians, poets, dreamers, religious pioneers, ardent missionaries, compulsive researchers and inventors read like an excursion in another world: "misfits," "eccentrics," "strange," "living before their day," "squares," "prudes," "other-worldings"—these are but a few epithets hurled their way. It is noteworthy that the throwers of such uncomplimentary verbal stones were diggers of ditches, menders of nets, tax collectors, calloused conformists, fair-weather religionists, or cowardly creatures who fought off the soul-stress which could have changed them into something other than plodders whose appetites demanded only meat and bread.

While it is an accepted axiom that no true works of art result from men out of breath, it is more strikingly true that no excelling

32

works of art are wrought by earth-bound sluggards or by belongers to lodge "togetherness"—that time-wasting modern heresy!

The nervous, dedicated steps of Handel still can be heard pacing midnight floors. A surging torrent of pent-up emotion kept probing and searching his life that memorable night. Wells of inspiration which reached all the way down to the vitals of a creative genius interplayed in him, stretching and stressing his imagination until he reached such feverish emotional ecstasy that God spoke in a vernacular of sharps and flats. The Hallelujah Chorus written that night became a milestone in the long succession of musical efforts to adore God and to exalt His name. His tension became a creative conduit through which God revealed the masterful music.

Michelangelo was a virtual prisoner to his task of decorating the high ceilings of Rome's churches. He endured nearly an enforced enslavement to complete a work which no other was considered capable of doing, disregarding health, convenience, adverse working conditions, public reaction, proper sleep. While mixing pigments of color in the stucco plaster as he shaped it on the ceiling of the Sistine Chapel, wet flecks would drop in his face and eyes; still, he stayed with the job. Loving dedication kept him at work. Little did he know that millions would stand in stiff-necked awe and admiration at this work of art which is unsurpassed.

Jesus of Nazareth hardly would have been called a "success" by most of His contemporaries. Yet, His singular life, viewed from any angle, reflects such embarrassing contrast to the lives of all other men that even the word "success" sounds like vulgar impiety. But, if verbal fools may rush in where angels fear to tread, the human part of Christ's life speaks with eloquent endorsement of this truth: the forces of strain and stress which destroy some men are the making of others. A tension-laden cross equaled more victory than all crowns of potentates combined.

Nor is the use of positive stress limited to the few devout souls who have a gift for such things. In any profession or work it can be employed with astounding results. Famous actors say that they go through several "heats" before going on stage. Sometimes two to three changes of clothes are involved before the initial ap-

33

pearance. Just another way of saying that mind and body are interplaying so that the subsequent performance will lift the audience above the wooden, mechanical level of acting.

Frank Lloyd Wright, remembered by many as an architectural nonconformist and pioneer, is said to have sat down before designing a new building and gotten himself into an emotional lather by imagining the scorn of his critics. Such an amalgam of anger, disgust, determination and piqued pride was just the right mixture to summon within him his own creative distinctives.

Many a preacher has given altitude and leverage to what otherwise would have been flat sermonic fruit by imagining he was "telling off his deacons." Deep inside all of us is a latent, dormant store of energies which, if let loose, could power this human machine in a way that most never dream is possible.

HARNESSING CREATIVE TENSION FOR LIFE'S UPHILL PULLS

A genuine Christian has an advantage over others since the nature of his faith is akin to crises much like warfare. Born in the tension of a crucifixion, it is part of a dying process that, though waning, is generating new life just as surely as new cells are hourly replacing those which have served their purpose and died off. This person with dual citizenship—one on earth and one in heaven—feels a compulsion from within which the unregenerate can never experience. The Christian interprets this tension as the handwork of God, a divine finger pointing to his pile of "coal" as potential energy. Feeling the surge of this inner power, the Christ-follower comes alive to the things that matter. His is a daily awareness that all things are not of equal importance; that some things matter not at all, and very few matter supremely. Singular action, cleanly scrubbed motives, dreams without apology, thoughts without shame, love without dissimulation—these are part and parcel of that Kingdom subject who is unafraid and unhampered. His life becomes a light that burns with incandescent brilliance at times; then, intentionally dimmed, the brilliance is reduced so as to accentuate the value and necessity of total illumination when needed.

34

Living 'twixt two straits, the child of God knows that such dualism is his normalcy, that reconciling double-citizenship is the only hope for qualitative effort in time or in eternity.

A PORTRAIT OF JESUS UNDER THE POWER OF DIVINE COMPULSION

Look at that one life in which gentle and violent forces were present. He could be as gentle as an elderly lady or as violent as a tornado. He could speak with the soothing consolation of a mother at eventide reassuring her first-born that night holds no horrors. Or, He could explode with the fury of an overactive volcano. Resenting the enslaving effects of wrong living, He minced no words while condemning it. Every fibre of His being was keyed to enraptured intensity as He foretold the doom of sinners. In His exaltation of the majesty of God, one would have thought that a hundred symphonic instruments had been called into action. Whether you trace His steps through the garden of intercession or walk with Him through the entangled paths of His wilderness of temptation, the same tension-mastering personality is there.

And He never ran from a fight. Knowing that a legion of resources was at His command, He calmly faced the music despite its discordant sound. Right here we could forego much of our tensive miseries, our midnights of unnecessary travail. Running from the very persons or circumstances which we should face never helps us. The mountain still raises its rocky head when finally in disgust the runner decides to return and face it.

When He was tempted to conform to Satan's pattern, Jesus was a seething maelstrom of emotion. Indignation, resentment, awareness did not swerve Him from knowing that God had not left Him alone to fight.

The Bible is replete with a stream of truth from His victories on the battlefield of Palestine: "I must work the works of him who sent me while it is day."—"Now is my soul troubled . . ." "And when he saw the multitudes, he was moved with compassion . . ." "Jesus wept,"—"Father, forgive them for they know not what they do." At every turn of the way He confronted the hectic human demands

35

and applied this wondrous truth of purpose and meaning. The temporal as well as the eternal called forth the "steam" of His energies. His was an index finger pointing out distinctions between time and eternity, shadow and substance, imaginary and real, the kingdoms of this world and the Kingdom of God, between actual and potential human nature. Just think of what He was able to accomplish in less than three years of public ministry. Without the advantage of longevity, extensive travel, or many earned degrees, He faced life with no reservations and overcame it. Yet, all travel agencies, university degrees and octogenarians combined have not affected the stream of human civilization as has this single, solitary Figure whose dynamic energies were harnessed and made to move under divine direction. Otherwise, how could He have met the deadline of Calvary?

HOW TO DEPLOY CREATIVE TENSION IN HUMAN BEHAVIOR

The acceptance of certain facts and the mastery of specific truths are essential if tension is to be servant rather than master. For instance, if a person is high-strung and moves in a one-speed fast gear, he must accept this fact as his normalcy, if glandular imbalance or self-induced stimuli are not in the picture. Moreover, the one-speed person should not always try to change to multiple speeds, or a transmission with a dozen variants. It is as normal and natural for such a high-geared person to move fast as for one who is congenitally slow to move at a snail's pace. Each was given his nature from his mother's womb and wishful thinking or envious attitude will do nothing to alter the facts. Expecting to change one's basic metabolism is as futile as believing that the ocean can be dried up with a mop. Can the leopard change his spots? No, because he doesn't need to do so. His spots, among other characteristics, make him a leopard.

I have witnessed too many people whose natural gifts were pronounced but whose old "up-and-at-'em" dispositions became addled and thwarted by the ill-prescribed throttles of tranquilizers. Prescribed and taken under medical direction for extreme, pathological tension, these may be a blessing, but eaten like aspirin to allay normal concerns which should be expressed in daily effort, their use is ill-advised. Who can think and act with fresh exuberance when he is clouded and befuddled by chemical controls?

Perhaps this is the proper place to stress the need of self-acceptance since it is in this acceptance that one becomes worthy of self-esteem.

Many people never really accept themselves; instead, they live in an inner world of painful envying, hounding self-effacement and devastating strife. Always trying to make themselves over by patterns of moral perfectionism, they rob their days of joy and peace in the futile process.

Any way one looks at it, life is a grindstone. Whether it grinds you down or polishes you up depends upon what you are made of. So much of the difficulty involved in this grinding process lies at the door of refusing to accept the person who lives inside our bodies. And despite the psychological compensation of egoism in self-expression, one may still be his own worst enemy. Many personal failures are more the result of inner collapse than of outward pressures.

This truth was pointed up recently when a Negro janitor found a roll of money on the floor under one of the desks in the foyer of a bank. Sneakily slipping it in his pocket, he thought of the vacation he hadn't been able to take for years, of the many things needed to furnish his house. His mind swirled in wild anticipation. But the next morning he brought the money to the office of the bank's president. "Why did you bring it to me?" the officer asked the Negro. "Well, you see, Sir, it's like this: As long as I live, I will have to live with myself and I don't want to live with a thief." This is the right way to deploy destructive tensions caused by creeping guilt or unconfessed wrong. "Know thyself" and "to thine own self be true," is by us wisdom needed no less than by the ancient Greeks.

AREAS OF TENSION NEEDING CREATIVE DIRECTION

When in the affairs of men there are lapses in civilization and man's slow journey out of the jungles slips backward, everyone is a loser. Midway in this twentieth century has occurred such a lapse —a lapse into the rutted sins of racial animosities, rationalized servitude, and the ironically erroneous notion that God looks with partiality on one race at the expense of another. Old seeds sown decades ago have germinated and are spreading their stench throughout the fields of the world. Anyone motivated by sincere sympathy and who exhibits a loving determination to bear the burdens of those who are downtrodden is regarded either as a deluded fool or a "communist fellow-traveler." The only reason Jesus was not called a communist was that neither the term nor the system of thought were known to His enemies. They called Him everything else. And most of His trouble occurred as a result of His effort to infuse a sense of decency and self-respect in the lost, the last, and the least. Such is the way that sin and sinners do their work. Unquestionable right and virtue always come in for scathing criticism by the lesser breeds.

Today's crosses are of different timber—not of aspen or Palestinian hardwood, but rather of the timber of ostracism, suspicion, rumor and half-truths. Held together by common ties of pathological ignorance, our would-be crucifiers sometimes are on official church boards, teach in some Sunday school classes, ferret their way to the purse strings of the finance committees; whenever possible, they gravitate to the more influential offices in congregational government with the avowed purpose of determining policy according to "their way of life."

We now have come to that time in history that demands our most intelligent consideration. Ours are not "peanut" problems; they stagger the imagination of world thinkers. This is the day for tall-standing people whose heads are in the sky and whose feet are on the ground. If history ever demanded upright posture, directional courage, objective outlook and common honesty, it is this moment, this day.

Yet, from the defiance and many of the utterances, threats and overtures, it appears that some human statue loses height all the time. The interpersonal relations of millions of people are at a standstill challenged by a "classless" totalitarianism on one hand

and a pale, effete religion of words on the other; little progress on this level is measured. Heat on the subject far outmeasures the light. Flush of tempers, raising of argumentative voices, and a never-ending parade of prejudices are common stock nowadays.

This frenetic state of things expresses itself in all sorts of absurd and cruel ways; for instance, the efforts to legislate morals. Just pass laws and expect all the issues to be settled! Many such laws become part of the existing problems rather than part of the solution. This is no plea for an irresponsible disregard of law; it is ready admission that legality is one thing, individual choice and initiative something else altogether. All of the easy mandates and edicts handed down from courts and councils notwithstanding, until individual men and women regard the human problem as being deeper, wider and bigger than mandates, the problem will continue to grow by apathetic attrition and foul-motived aggravation. Sin is as real in a white face and heart as in a colored face and heart. Real blackness is that smut which pigments the human mind and soul; and the only effective bleach known is the blood of Jesus Christ. This is why the issue is not so much one of race as it is of theology, since all the grandiose schemes for improving human conditions fall flat unless they commence and end with the unmotivated love of Jesus Christ.

In this orb of racial strife, made more poignant by masses on the march, old empires crumbling, and new dynasties like hot-house plants rising overnight, where does the Church of Jesus Christ stand? Who is proclaiming that this racial tension can become a creative step instead of a pathologically defeative stumbling block? A few . . . not many! And that to the undoing of all who love freedom, the Lord and a future worth experiencing.

Look at the disconcerting facts: nearly three billion people alive today with 140,000 babies being born every twenty-four hours. This is a net in round numbers of fifty million per year! It took the human race from Adam to recent time to reach the two billion mark; it will require but a few years more for the three billion mark to be reached. This means more people, more hunger, hatred, wars, lust, greed and misery. Just how much more of each it will mean depends to an appreciable degree upon the urgency we show in giving direction to the present waves of race tension.

Genuine Christians must bring their prejudices under the sway of the will of God. After the initial experience of salvation, there comes that long and laborious process known as conversion in which the will of the individual ego becomes harmonized with the Master's. Punching the clock on entering the office at the beginning of a day is merely the first of many acts composing a day's work. So with those who follow Christ. The initial act must be first in a long series of battles in exorcism.

Prejudice is a slant of the mind and heart to the left of the fact; an opinion formed without all the facts in hand. Search as you will, the annals of history record no instances in which God was able to accomplish any worthwhile Kingdom advance through people who remained galvanized to prejudice and bigotry.

But make no mistake about it: yielding the right-of-way to God in an area where many adamantly swear they are right takes dimensions of soul which few possess. It is common knowledge to the casual observer than many well-informed people can speak dispassionately on most subjects, but when it comes to the race issue, they suddenly black out to all reason, coolness and, in some cases, even manners or fairness. I have talked with many possessing graduate degrees whose "pro-con" logic point out the many related angles of a given subject, but who start seeing black the moment human relations are mentioned. What irony! What inexcusable inconsistency!

Prejudices are caused by many conditioning influences: early training, dislike on the part of parents for certain colors, specific people, superstitions and the like. Usually we fear what or whom we do not understand. Thus, one race is taught to discredit and distrust another; a republic, steeped in propaganda, conditions its people against other nations; one religion often consumes valuable time slanting its adherents against all other religions. It is quite easy to build up prejudice toward one's own denomination or, for that matter, the Bible. Reading the Word of God with the grey spectacles of theological bias, permitting the record to say just what one wants it to say while conveniently overlooking the passages which would set the reader straight in his interpretation, is the way of many. The hop-skip-and-jump style interpretation never permits the authoritative Word to speak its full message.

Look at the prejudicial attitude toward the church by many a worldly sinner. Such believe the church to be some sort of necessary evil, a carry-over from days when it was believed that the world was flat and when priestcraft ruled science. This attitude today, as much as any other, explains the absence of millions from the household of faith. Just such prejudice blinds them to the abiding values which they so vehemently deny.

If anyone still labors under the misapprehension that Jesus was a county-seat reformer, condoning the "chosen people" myth, encouraging the local precinct neighbors at the expense of the foreigner, then let him take another look at the record. That Nazarene made a Samaritan—a half-breed—the hero in His parable of neighborliness. When it came to helping and loving people, Jesus had a way of seeing the Syrophenician woman, encouraging the Roman centurion, accepting favors of a Cyrenian, compassionately healing a Gadarene, instructing the visiting Greeks, denouncing, yet directing, the Judeans. In Him there was no East nor West, North nor South and every man born in the divine image came within the province of His redemptive love. I am sure that if we are to be like Him, our prejudices will have to go—go all the way to Calvary and there be nailed to the tree. Only then can there be resurrective newness of mind and spirit. The solution to this sin that grips our nation concerning man's relation to man lies where it always has: in a regenerated mind and soul that discovers the simplest direction to God is in turning right and going straight.

But if we continue to put the new wine of a transforming gospel in old wine-skins that are creased and wrinkled by many summers of hate and fear, we shall not meet God's schedule or urgency. To ask, "What would Jesus do?" is far closer to the point than asking what the legislature would do, or any other assemblage. What Christ would do is exactly what He did! There is no guesswork about that fact. And we have the record to prove it. He so ve-

41

hemently resented the traffic in human nature, the travesties on justice, man's inhumanity to man, that He revolted with crushing indignation.

Basically, when it is all said and done, this issue is religious after all. For religion penetrates every facet of life: how one makes his living, equal opportunities for education, play, worship—all. A jolting criticism struck our smug complacency when one uncharitably contended that "We need to be shaken out of the magnolias." If the hand that would shake is muscled and motivated by love, all right, let us be shaken. But if it is merely the censorious hand of self-appointed Pharisees whose complacency and our double standards contradict our sweet-scented magnolias, then let the shaking wait. The trouble is that God can't get a word in on this subject since we are always vocalizing our own persuasions. Maybe if He could be heard, He would ask us, "What color was Jesus, anyway?" Or better still, perhaps He would remind that among the reasons they crucified Him was the fact that Christ must have been color-blind!

Of course, for the moment, there is an easy way out: to bypass the whole controversy by saying religion shouldn't deal with such matters anyway, that these had better be left to other provinces, and to retreat into the comfortable, nauseating "security" of religion. When Christianity beats such a cowardly retreat, it doesn't remotely resemble its Founder.

One can do what my fledgling preacher friend from Kentucky did when, after having preached half a dozen sermons in his new church, a Diotrephes who loved to have preëminence among the brethren came to him and asked him to soft-pedal any controversial issue. The next Sunday the young minister pedaled with a thirty-two foot pipe the obligation of every Christian to shoot straight with God concerning his money. That night the sermon dealt with the explosive subject of divorce. After the service a dozen men "waited" on the fearless young prophet.

"We want our church to be popular, to attract people and we don't want it to be a storm center of controversy, where folks get their feelings hurt. After all, we've got to raise a lot of money to

42

pay off the old debt and we don't want people to become divided."

"But what shall I preach then?" my bewildered friend asked them.

"Preach on, well, on anything that won't make the folks mad. Preach on the Jews—there ain't one in a hundred miles of here."

Will we fall victim to a similar fate? Or will we let the Son of God speak to our hearts with His scathing, dynamic, prejudice-exorcising logic? In the process He thus would assure us that we are on the way to glory in fellowship with the redeemed from every country and climate.

The legend that will not die in postwar Germany contends that Hitler's infamous edict, required reading from the pulpits of Germany, stated, "Those of you who have Jewish blood in your veins on your fathers' side, get up and leave the service now. It doesn't matter how long you have held membership in this church, what office you have held, or your personal objections. Leave and do not return. You are no longer welcome. We are trying to give rise to an Aryan race, the only one worthy of inhabiting the earth." Hearing the weak, vacillating preachers who were more conscious of their own skin and its safety, the congregation could hardly believe their ears. But surely enough, two or three on the main floor, one from the choir loft, and one in the side balcony, rose, bowed their heads and went out. Then the edict continued: "Those of you who have Jewish blood in your veins on your mothers' side, you too leave and never return. It matters not how long you have been here or what you have contributed." This time, half a dozen left from the stunned crowd. The legend says that the Jew hanging on the cross over the altar, high above the choir loft looking down on *those who stayed*, came down and went out! Usually He does, you know, when He is insulted in His own house.

Creative tension—yes, even in such a dizzying storm as the race issue.

The Sin of Worry

2

You can't change the past, but you can ruin a perfectly good present by worrying over the future.

"Why be distracted about your life ...?"—Jesus Christ

INTO THE STREETS of a large, American city a middle-aged man was sent on a strange mission. Armed with two sacks of silver dollars, he was instructed to give one silver dollar to every person who appeared to be happy. Early in the morning he was on the job near the depots, office buildings, bus terminals, busy thoroughfares and street corners. After working all day, he had given away only $739. Why so few in a city of two million people? Was his conception of what a happy person looks like too critical? Or is happiness something deep inside that cannot be detected by a casual observer?

More of the answer lies in the fact that we are not a happy lot. Worry, fear, anxieties travel up and down the avenues of our minds so constantly that happiness has little chance of survival with most of us. The preoccupied, fast-walking, nervous-glancing, eager beaver doesn't leave the impression with anyone that happiness is his or her daily fare. The French have a word called "sabot" meaning wooden shoe. In their efforts to compensate for poor wages some years ago in industrial plants, the French workers threw wooden shoes in the factory wheels. The resultant wreckage of the machine was considered ample compensation by the workers. From that word we get our English word "sabotage." Human nature knows something of that same process: it throws little wooden shoes into the delicate mechanism of the human mind—the shoes of worry which clog the delicate wheels of balance and health.

ANATOMY OF WORRY—THE UGLY COMPONENTS

Thought, so essential to rational living, becomes obsessive activity. Preoccupation that will not turn an issue loose turns on itself, re-evaluating, reweighing, reappraising. Such is the rutted road of a worrying disposition. Like infection in the blood stream, the virus of a fretted mind can make the whole organism ill. Worry is concern working overtime. It is an inordinate attitude of involvement. So long as a river follows its normal course it can bring blessings to those who live on its banks. But when rising to flood-tide, the river can bring havoc and destruction on all things living near its ribbon of liquid death. So worry, well-intentioned, starting out as desirable concern, gets out of its banks and becomes a rude intruder into every facet of the mind, exercising an egotistical insistence that all issues bend to its demands, every mood be conditioned by its imperatives. So long as worry is given intelligent direction, it can turn the turbines of thought, intelligent decision and will power. But let it loose to run like an ungoverned motor, and the results are monotonously familiar. Running on late into the night instead of shutting off at the end of the day, this ruinous process extracts an unbelievable tax in joy, health, energy and perspective.

CARE AND WORRY IN DISTINCTION

> *Worry is like a rocking-horse; it keeps*
> *you going, but it gets you nowhere.*

Many fail to distinguish between intelligent concern on one hand and lopsided concern on the other. The advice of Jesus given in the Sermon on the Mount does not say, "Take no thought for tomorrow," as one translation contends. As a matter of fact, most of what He said added up to exactly the opposite. Taking thought for tomorrow is the essence of discipleship. Where would the church—or the nation—be, if thought were not taken for the future? His parables about the soils, the talents, the man building a tower—yes, most of them fit under the heading of thought-taking in proper

45

degree about the future. Nor did He say, "Be not anxious about tomorrow." Never did Jesus demand the impossible on man's part. And to fail to demonstrate anxiety is an impossibility. He did say, "Be not distracted about tomorrow." And that is a different process altogether. Distraction is that befuddled state of affairs when one tries to go in two directions at once. Arriving at a "Y" in life's roads, distraction would have the traveler going forward on neither road.

Intelligently oriented care is directed concentration. Worry is more like inflammation than concentration. Nowhere did the Saviour imply that people who follow Him are to be a shifting, unprepared lot, floating in naïve detachment. Such would not be faith but foolishness. Yet, after a man has sat down and figured the cost of his tower and started construction, then to refigure, reappraise, and never permit the mind that security which comes when one has done his best is merely to drop in that old rut of worry and to rob the construction of its fine, potential joy.

THE SCOPE AND MAGNITUDE OF THE WORRYING PROCESS

The familiar office caricature of a moronic-looking man with snaggled teeth, crossed eyes, and demented face saying, "Worry, who me?" is hardly representative of the multi-millions who are guilty of daily worrying. Approximately three million Americans get ulcers every year, and ten thousand deaths are caused by this disease. More people between thirty-five and fifty have ulcers—the years of peak average earning power. Men are more susceptible to ulcers than women. Few, if any, age groups are exempt. Once there was a time when young people were too carefree, too engrossed in a thousand-and-one pursuits to be accused of worrying. Other than escalating emotions of a love affair a month, the battles among the young were mere local skirmishes. Not so, anymore. Among the ulcer sufferers in the mid-twentieth century are teen-agers and pre-teen-agers. Fingernail eaters are not limited to any age. Single people have their own peculiar corpus of worrying, while married folk plow their own acres of indulgent worries. The saint and sinner, rich and poor, illiterate and educated, young and old number among those who seem to be on an endless binge of feverish worrying.

Proof of this contention is in easy evidence. Our health picture is a good starting place. Despite the fact of rich, vitamin-heavy diets, America's health is comparatively shoddy. One would think that folks who slept in the softest beds, lived in the most comfortable homes, drank the purest milk, and enjoyed the most varied exercise would be the healthiest. But in a recent contest where American youth were pitted against their European counterparts, America's boys and girls made out poorly. Ranking often as low as fifth and sixth to their across-the-sea cousins, the over-all facts leave much to be desired. In many of the low-rating contestants, often there was lack of a sound, healthy attitude.

Fifty-one per cent of all hospitalized patients in our nation are suffering from other than organic diseases. Many, if not most, of these fit somewhere in that vague but specific province of inordinate concern called worry. The nation's seven thousand hospitals usually are filled to capacity with waiting lists for the better private rooms. The same institutions last year spent more than ten billion dollars employing more people than the car makers and oil refiners combined! Think of it: all the apparent ingredients for sound health, yet all that sickness. Is it any wonder that we must label the monster of worry a sin?

In a recent year there were 37,000 suicides in America. Would you attempt to guess in which month more people take their lives than any other? Cold, bleak January? Windy, changing March? No. May! The month of flowers, bright, fresh sunlight, singing birds and new intimations of immortality—May. Worry is a killer that respects neither the person immediately involved nor those interwoven in his life by love's involvements.

The mushrooming of drugstores indicates a national trend of misery and unhappiness. In a small, county-seat town in the South the two main factories are an aspirin producer and a commercial fertilizer plant. In the years from 1956 through 1958, the tonnage of aspirin exceeded the fertilizer tonnage! This incredible fact

47

speaks of a national headache, the greater portion of which generates in a worrying mind. Tranquilizers, sleeping tablets, "pep" pills and a host of other crutches point accusingly at our poorly ordered lives. There are throngs of citizens who could neither stay awake in the daytime nor go to sleep at night without their ever-present prescription bottle handy.

Even an amateur's prognosis of this condition is gloomy. If the present trend to worry over every major decision is not checked and reversed, the next generations will know more about psychiatrists, psychologists, counselors, and shock therapy than they will about rowing a boat, char-broiling a steak or simple arithmetic. Worse still: the unborn generations are apt to be a family of emotional misfits whose lives are little more than walking civil wars—a host of psychotics, schizophrenics and otherwise miserable souls. The few reputable centers that we have today for treating the emotionally ill will in a few years have waiting lists a decade long.

THE ROLE OF THE CHRISTIAN CHURCH IN MENTAL ILLNESS

It no longer is sufficient for the church to say, "Come to Jesus," and mean by such a statement that all the problems will be solved in coming. As a matter of fact, many of the problems just begin with that process. The problems of becoming a new creature, exorcising evil disposition, and cultivating an emotional system worthy of the name involves endless regimen under the right leadership. Herein the church has closed its eyes to one of the greatest mission fields in existence: the field of mentally disturbed people. Chronic worriers who need guidance out of the swamp of self-destruction, millions who are mired-up in their minds, must have recourse to some helping hand. About 80 per cent of those who need professional help with these functional ills cannot afford it financially. If they could, there still would be less than half the professional personnel needed. Such being the condition, the next best way of helping these people is for the church to provide at least semi-professional guidance. Who more than ministers should have, not

48

only a sympathetic outlook, but some know-how in counseling the mentally disturbed? Without some professional training, efforts to help in this field can become a part of the problem instead a part of the solution. Among the assignments in the commission which Jesus gave to the early disciples was, ". . . and as you go *heal* the sick. . . ." It is to the discredit of the record that "faith" healers and religious quacks have scared the rest away from our responsibility in this area of ever-mounting, pathetic need. At least the larger churches must make provisions for meeting some of the increasing bulk of human emotional needs. Preaching sermons on healthy minds is one thing; pointing a kind finger of love toward the preventive paths is another. Both are in order: warning and rebuke, encouragement and chastisement. But I fear the heavier diet has run along the accusative line. There is no greater mission field than the millions who make up the twilight world of chronic, miserable worriers. And if the field that Jesus looked across was white with harvest two thousand years ago in a country smaller than one of our smallest states, what about the field of today's world where nearly three billion people live? And as the world's area shrinks by overcrowding, the need for honestly facing this problem will be pointed up in sharper relief. Tragically, our concern over its present dimensions is such a paltry thing that the future portends nothing more than gloom unless there is a revolutionary change from our present attitude.

THE EFFECTS OF WORRY ON THE BODY'S NERVOUS SYSTEM

In certain respected medical circles there is a growing conviction that most, if not all, sickness is traceable to one source: tensive stress. Pioneering in this belief, Dr. Hans Selye points to his Stress Hypothesis, exploring all types of organic diseases that have some functional affinities. His findings are near-revolutionary. Maybe some day the only equipment of the medic when he makes his calls will be the Bible after all! I have the deepest sense of gratitude for all those historic souls who have burned the midnight oil

49

to discover precious radium, sulfates, and the whole wondrous spectrum of "miracle" drugs. Still, my gratitude does not blur the fact that man's deepest maladies cannot be reached by a surgeon's scalpel nor a practitioner's pills.

What does worry do to your health? In a word, it can wreck it just as surely as cancer. This fact explains and defines the nature of Christian responsibility toward one's body. "Know ye not that the body is the temple of the soul?"—not a shack or hovel, but a temple: an edifice of beauty, resilient and tough. Since God made it, He entailed responsibility for its upkeep. Any activity that degrades, limits, impairs or wrecks the body—even that rationalized activism in the name of organized religion—is not justified by one's sense of values. We have a stewardship to our corpuscles as well as to our cash.

Take a look at the interior: three little glands that do not weigh a third of an ounce all put together make the difference between health and sickness. The pituitary, thyroid and adrenal glands work in concert like a well-rehearsed trio to give tone, energy and balance. Nothing short of a miracle is observed as they secrete their small amounts of chemicals in the stream of life. If one sits in a draft and becomes chilled, automatically a whole battalion of invisible soldiers is rushed to command the heart to pick up its beat and warm the body in compensation for the cool air coming through the window.

If infection sets in at any point of the body, automatically the tiny sentinels set up guard around the infected area causing festering and healing. The human heart, a little organ about the size of one's fist, beats a hundred thousand times a day. When one begins to worry, that already hard-worked organ is forced to work overtime. The rate is accelerated, the pace goes unabated. Think of it: one tiny organ without a single minute's vacation from the cradle to the grave, an organ that pumps enough blood every twenty-four hours, to fill a tank car on a railroad siding. At best, under relaxed conditions the heart has enough work to do. But let the temper rise, the body become exercised unnecessarily in anxiety and worrisome fears, and the old ticker starts pounding like a trip hammer.

It all means that several hundred extra gallons of blood have to be pumped through a plumbing system the diameter of whose pipes is comparable to the diameter of a large needle or a small pencil.

Actually the many technical terms—coronary thrombosis, occlusion, and the like—are ways of saying that the heart and its system were given too severe a beating in the jig of life—a type of functional suicide. Death often is just the last turning off of the switch on the way out of the room of life. There isn't anything wrong with the wiring system. If the tread is taken off the mental tires by skidding, brake-riding and "scratching" off to meet some absurd deadline or quota, a blowout is inevitable—inevitable for saint as well as sinner.

RELATION OF WORRY TO HURRY—THE PAGAN PACE

A direct nexus exists between worry and hurry. One depends upon the other for its pace; as a matter of fact, worry in all probability determines the frantic pace in which we hurry from this to that as though life were a marathon to see who could beat the other to the grave. The Bible contains an embarrassing reminder: "The race is not to the swift nor the spoils to the strong." A nervous jig does not determine efficiency; most times, the very opposite is true. Our old military jargon, "Hurry up and wait," still is common practice for many civilians as well. To go one worse, we hurry up and worry up. Who pays any attention nowadays to the Old Testament wisdom: "He that believeth shall not make haste"? But the production manager, the efficiency experts, the statistical maniacs all believe that making haste is the essence of making success, that motion is bound to be progress—and away we go.

The fact that the decade between the ages of forty-five and fifty-five claims more lives proportionately than the two older decades seems to be a weak deterrent to the pace and process of hurrying. It may be irksome therapy, but it can prove a boon to the day if, when the amber light is always turning at every other block and you think some prankster came in the night and jimmied up the lights just so they will turn against your driving, you stop, think, and remember: "He that believeth shall not make haste." For that one moment of emotional inventory-taking the soul can catch up with the body and the union is a happy one—a rare thing in this day of whirling dervishes.

Right here we might face up to a hounding admission: one cannot have intensity of experience and permanence of duration; he cannot burn the candle at both ends and in the middle too without consuming the candle. The luxury of having one's cake and eating it too is more than this world promises or more than anybody deserves. To choose a sensible moderation of pace, which in itself is insulation against worrying, is more a guarantee for longevity than any other single factor. Which is the more delightful experience: to drive your car at a leisurely pace through open countryside, noticing the unfolding view of beauty, or to ride a fast passenger train where much of the scenery is obscured by subterranean tunnels, swishing light posts, and dizzying curves? Getting nothing more than a zip, zip, snatch of view is a poor way to see anything. But when one determines his own speed, the wonderful panorama unfolds in an orderly sequence of magnificence.

A 365-day clock is wound once a year because of its slow, measured, staccato rhythm. But a rackety, nervous alarm clock must be wound every night. For centuries waltz music has been the favorite music of multitudes, whereas "bebop" is as short-lived as a college athlete's glory. Hurry and worry join hands to form an infamous duet whose tune is discord and whose toll is immeasurable.

WHY WORRY IS WICKED

When Jesus referred to sin and sinning, He usually used a word that graphically describes a familiar process. It was the picture of an archer with drawn bow with arrow pointed toward the center of his target. Upon releasing the arrow, it shoots off to one side, missing the bull's-eye completely. The word *hamartia* means more literally "missing the mark." Therefore, any process, activity or event that causes a Christian to miss his mark in life is sinning.

Worry will come as close to diverting the arrow from the central purpose of God as any known activity. But some will object, Granted that worry destroys much of life's sweetness, but isn't it too strong to say that worry is a sin? Hardly. Any functioning attitude that ignores the nature of divine promise while denuding life of zest and certainty is nothing less than sin. So this nagging, involved mental process is more than weakness: it is wickedness. How can God comfortably reside in a soul that distrusts and aggravates every certainty by the ever-present conditionals: if, maybe, perhaps, probably? Who can picture Jesus of Nazareth permitting His mind to be clogged by ten thousand overriding issues of worry? To say that His concern sounded the depths of human emotions is an understatement. But to conclude that He went off in all directions at once, all lathered up over the outcome of human actions, is to misrepresent Him completely.

> Just take this comfort in your soul,
> In the midst of your worries and frets:
> The football never could score a goal
> Were it not for the kicks it gets.
>
> —Anonymous

AREAS OF WORRY

The Inconsequentials—Things That Do Not Matter

An area claiming a lion's share of energy and mental effort is one that is least deserving: the realm of a thousand-and-one inconsequentials. Little issues, finite claims, gnats'-heel-size arguments, pint-size controversies—these are the little forces that damage the vines of superlative living. If one would take stock at the end of his day and list the conduits that siphoned off most of his energies, caused most of the heartaches, the results would reveal a maddening picture. It is not the major battles, the higher hills that claim the ghastly number of casualties, but the aggravating, incessant inconsequentials. Most of our lives are summed up, not in epochal events, but in a succession of little occurrences and relatively unim-

53

portant happenings. Mastery of these is far more essential than successful handling of the few big events and occasions.

Part of the answer to the need for more time in order to do the things we would like to do is not in trying to find that magic twenty-fifth hour. Nor is it in juggling one rationalism with another. Time? Why, we have all the time there is, all the time there ever has been. It is what we do with our time that matters. To attain a serene life in the midst of a cauldron of confusion one must possess a sense of the predominanting values, an understanding of what really matters—in the long run—with God; then, with the discipline of a Spartan, one must give himself to these few essential things. This will be a strugggle, with many distractions: the corresponding secretary of the "let's plant petunias on the abandoned lot" society will plead urgently for cooperation; dues and attendance at the Secret Society for the Social Idle and Ignorant will demand unswerving loyalty at every meeting; competition in the flower arranging sorority will produce its embryonic ulcers. If life must be used up in a multiplicity of verbs, why not let a sense of values at least decide which verbs will be the consumers? Surely the answer is not in more going, nor in more belonging, and—perish the thought—not in more togetherness! Conversely, the answer resides in that hardheaded wisdom which admits, without cynicism, that most of the things that drive, annoy and dismay us don't count for two ounces on the scales of eternity. Why should they be marked as weighing tons on the scale of time?

It is an irony of the first magnitude that adult men and women can get so fussed up over five-cent values, so inflamed over dime-store premises. Think of it: ten billion brain cells focused on a ten-cent issue. When asked what gave him the most trouble during his hike from Seattle to Savannah, an old man thought for a while. Was it the constantly changing terrain with its steep hills and curving mountains? Or the hot, humid air of the deserts? Was it the whirl of passersby who registered no thought of offering him a seat in their cars had he not wanted to walk? Or perhaps it was the unpredictable weather with its alternating dryness and rain. Just what? Finally he said, "I suppose the one thing that gave me more annoyance than anything else was the sand in my shoes." Tiny grains of grit can abrade like an emery wheel. So in the stroll of the mind's adventure, puny but irritating particles of worry will rob the journey of its pleasantness.

Worry Over Things That Cannot Be Changed

> Worry is an old man with bended head,
> Carrying a load of feathers which he thinks are lead.
>
> —Anonymous

Alexander the Great is reported to have worried over the fact that ivy would not grow in Babylon. But I do not have to leave my neighborhood to find people worrying over the same thing.

Man's powers have challenged most of the forces he has encountered on his long trek from primitive conditions. Defying the impossible, he has flung his efforts into conquering deserts, draining swamps, isolating viruses, reproducing nature, and now reaching toward the heavens to shrink the spatial universe. Still, there are some things that man has not been able to do. He cannot make the sun stand still, nor can he change the color of his skin. Making a square circle is not his forte. He cannot put the gears of history in reverse. Nor can man stay the hand of death when it has doubled up its fist to knock on a door.

Now to worry about any of these things is absurd! Worrying over the things that cannot be changed is stupid. We should try to change the things that need to be changed without the additional encumbrance of fearful anticipation and endless procrastination. Letting chores pile up unnecessarily calls for tripled effort and additional mental tax when finally the piles are lowered by applied energies.

Knowing the difference between that which is unchangeable and that which is subject to change is a difficult, yet prime necessity. At least such knowledge will prevent one's hammering away on unnecessary boulders, thereby conserving energy and time for the needed blows on the right targets.

55

Orientals have an attitude that amounts to semi-holy resignation. Their attitude is epitomized in this saying: A stork has long legs while a duck's legs are short. As one can neither shorten the legs of the stork nor lengthen the legs of the duck, acceptance of the two conditions as they are is a type of resignation which humanity must master.

THE MERCY OF TIME AS AID IN ACCEPTING THE UNCHANGEABLES

When asked his favorite passage of Scripture, an old Negro farmer who had seen many winters—most of them filled with trouble—answered, "My favorite passage is: 'And it came to pass.'" Thinking that he had forgotten the rest of the sentence, his inquisitor wanted to know why that short phrase was his favorite. "You see, it's like this," he said. "Nothing that happens to you in life comes to stay; it all came to pass on. Yes, my favorite is 'And it came to pass.'" Such distilled wisdom would serve more of us if we would but let it tone our discordant lives when we come up against things over which we have no control.

For years a small wooden plaque has rested on the edge of my study desk on which is printed four simple, sobering words: "And this shall pass." Each day I am reminded of the transitoriness of life and its fleeting, one-way traffic. The total impact of the motto is not frenetic desperation; rather, it helps keep the load of life from becoming top-heavy.

When one reaches that mental plateau where he can regard with passive detachment things which for years he considered impossible to live with, he then is becoming a candidate for superlative living.

The Inevitables

Many worry habitually about things that are inevitable in the course of human events: things that are going to happen despite one's attitude one way or the other. It must be granted that some things once deemed inevitable no longer fit into such a category. Most formerly fatal diseases which have been conquered by medical

56

research were once considered either demonic possession, inherent sinfulness or the ill omen of the gods. Now, thank God, we know better. However, the basic list of the inevitables remains unchanged —like growing old, for instance. A multimillion-dollar business each year tries to prevent nature from wrinkling, graying, stooping, atrophying. In some cases, a pretty good job is accomplished. Artificial hair, teeth, limbs, eyes—all speak of modern effort to change the inevitable process of aging. Parenthetically, research along this line is one of the more interesting prongs of human thought. It is altogether possible that within this century scientists will have isolated the ultra-microscopic agents in the life flow which cause cells and tissue to age and die. Until that day, we must reckon with the universal fact that while we can adorn old age, season it with wisdom which younger years cannot do, nonetheless, so long as we breathe we breathe in closer proximity to a casket each day.

When a brash teen-ager asked an elderly man why he was so old, the octogenarian answered realistically, "Why, if I were not old I would be dead." A three-line prayer portrays a wholesome attitude toward the inevitables: "God, give me courage to change the things which I can change; the patience to accept the things which I cannot change, and the sense to know the difference."

The list of inevitables is longer than the do-it-yourself school will admit. Weather, first capricious then soothing, still has the last word. Death sooner or later comes to all, the hand of resentment and the miracle drugs notwithstanding.

THE CHRISTIAN CURE FOR PAGAN WORRY

Now that something of the scope and magnitude of this negative art of worrying has been surveyed along with the areas wherein it is practiced, we turn to look at the cures for worry. Those mentioned belong almost exclusively to professing Christians. The resources available to them are not available to the unregenerate by virtue of his unestablished relationship to God through Jesus Christ.

Give to Life Your Best—and to God Leave the Rest

Though elemental in sound, this truth is not easy to practice. Many do not try hard enough while others try too hard. Superfluous effort can limit the performance and encourage unnecessary mental activity. Not even God expects of us more than our best. For several centuries there have thrived sects in Christianity that taught and preached a kind of moral perfectionism. Trying to dot every "i" and cross every "t" in behavior, they denuded life of many joys— joys that were otherwise innocent if their attitude could have been a positive one. Much of this specious theology stemmed from a mis- understanding of one word which Jesus used. The admonition in His statement, "Be ye therefore perfect," was taken to mean moral perfectionism. As a result, everything that spoke of materialistic pleasure was immediately assigned to the nether region of evil. The word Jesus used for "perfect" also means "mature" . . . "You be therefore mature." The utilitarian concept hasn't the slightest kin- ship with a negative, woebegone emasculation of every activity so familiar in our day. Yet, thousands refuse to believe the literal translation given above and continue to be engrossed in the im- possible burden of moral perfectionism. The naked truth of the matter is that one who had kept all the 613 do's and don'ts of Judaistic theology failed to pass the higher test of spiritual values in the eyes of Jesus. If the same time spent in trying to be good were spent in learning to love, lift and live, this world would be much nearer the Kingdom than it is.

A chronic worrier should feel no reticence in admitting his need for help from others. If he has a trusted friend, then he should rely on him for counsel. Usually one who wraps up his difficulty inside makes it worse. Admitting one's need for help is not a sign of weakness; it is a short-cut to strength.

Much of the misery that is endured daily is unnecessary. With a giant-size chunk of pride and the current wave of humanistic "do-it-yourselfness," we rush to work, into classroom, factory, and field with the tonnage of unconfessed burdens hanging around our hearts and heads. With our tiny shovels in hand we furiously start throwing the dirt to both sides. Then evening comes and most of what we had imagined should have been accomplished remains undone. The night becomes a ghastly stage whereon self whips self for not doing what a worrying imagination erroneously set for it to do.

Now, God sees the pile of dirt that we wanted to move. With a fleet of bulldozers at His disposal, He would like to send them to help our self-sufficient efforts—not as a substitute for our effort but as a supplement. Our little shovels are important; each must move his share of the dirt, because God will do nothing at all for a person that the person can do for himself. But it is no insult to one's ego to admit that he can't move all the dirt or wash all the pots and pans by himself. The graveyards of the nation would have a decidedly smaller population if more had learned this obvious lesson.

Because of hyper-self-criticism, emotional knots are tied even harder. We are our worst enemies when we drive ourselves beyond the point of sensible endurance, either in expectation of achievement records or in demanding unusual performance. Your best may not be another's best—nor should it be. The beauty about Christian discipleship is its individuality. In the parable of the talents the one-talent possessor was expected to do no more proportionately than the five-talent person. Had he done his best, the Master would have spoken the same rewarding words, "Well done . . . enter thou into the joy of thy Lord." Unfortunately history records only the home runs, not the fannings out. Yet, God looks at the quality of effort more than He looks at the score. And while a certain amount of self-criticism is in order, too much will impede the progress it is designed to accelerate.

Cultivate the Art of Detachment

The ancient Greeks developed a wonderful stop-valve against mental hazards. They were constantly battered by ideas, conflicting philosophies and natural cruelties. As a buffer against extreme misfortune, their art of detachment became an operative wonder. By way of definition, this detachment was a conscious effort to sit in the bleachers, passing judgment on the pace and quality of the performance in the arena, and at the same time to be a participant. This dual role, played in proper proportion, is a unique type of salvation: participator and spectator in the same person. If we do not have this attitude, it is impossible to judge the quality of our action. Obviously, life degenerates for the critic who only sits on the sidelines. But if one is a constant participator, and never a spectator, where along the line can one judge any-thing—least of all, himself?

The absence of some such working philosophy means that one sees the jumbled parts of life without ever clearly discerning even the profile of the whole. Hence, a functioning atheism sweeps the countryside; the puzzles remain unassembled. Some of the parts seem out of place and try as we may, there often seems no place for them to fit.

This fragmented outlook on life must come in for its share of the blame in the matter of worrying. For instance, one year may be a series of adverse forces such as drought, flood, tornadoes, or some similar occurrence. But shall we then conclude that Nature is one fiasco after another, never following any semblance of order or pattern? A brief span of time may show prosperity alternating with poverty—but neither is to be regarded as the norm. When an average is sought on the graph of events, it will be found that worry in spurts is no more justified than elation in spurts. An honest line to determine the nature of things would bisect ups and downs, in circumstances, high and low moments, good and bad feelings, religious fervor and religious chill, age and youth, promi-nence and obscurity. All these lines must be considered, since life has its share of each. Otherwise, a person would not be chari-table to himself, his God and his world when trying to conclude what it is all about. The ability to look at oneself in action, to hold self in proper rein, is the ability to prevent burning out or rust-ing out.

Once again, an Oriental sage aptly exemplified this art of de-tachment when relating his neighbor's attitude. His Chinese friend had one horse and one son. When his horse strayed off, his friends came in and sympathetically said, "We are sorry that you have had such bad luck." The farmer calmly replied, "Was it bad luck?" A few days later the horse came home, bringing three wild horses with him. "We rejoice with you in your good fortune," his neighbors remarked. "Is it good luck?" the strange Chinese replied. When questioned about his lack of sorrow and elation, he explained that his only son, while riding one of the wild horses, fell and broke his leg. The neighbors again expressed sympathy. The farmer then pointed out that the broken leg was not bad luck, since a war broke out and because of his injured leg the boy was not called into service. And on it goes. What is bad and what is good? One thing is certain and sure: everything that happens in life should be regarded with a degree of detachment, lest one's emotional system become an elevator rising and falling with every changing condition. This is not to propose an attitude of stoicism, that icy indifference which takes grief and joy in the same wooden stride. Actually, that type of rigidity is the worst sort of hypocrisy, wherein one remains unmoved outwardly while inwardly emoting. "Rejoice with them that do rejoice, and weep with them that weep"—this is evidence of honest empathy. But let there be a citadel deep within the recesses of the soul where external events—and worry—cannot intrude.

Reënforce the Inner Braces to Resist the Outer Pressures

There may be little one can do to slacken the constant pounding of outward pressures but the inner braces of resistance can be reënforced. Few signs on the horizon of civilization indicate any slackening of the external pressures; every indication is that they are becoming more intensified, more organized, more stubborn. But man can cultivate muscles in his mind and soul that will give leverage to his efforts in withstanding the bombardment.

The truth of the matter is that too many are cowards when it comes to facing these pressures. A person who won't put up a decent fight, but surrenders his swords without even a meager effort, is no candidate for leadership.

Real evil consists in keeping the soul locked up, never per-

61

mitting its freedom. Like a butterfly imprisoned in its silky cell, held back from potential flight, human personality can be locked in a narrow, worrying prison. Emancipation of self from within, a revolution in the soul of man—then the wells of living waters will flow!

When asked by his close friend why he voted for a particular bill in Congress—one obviously shy on ethical content—the wily politician answered, "But Bill, you can't imagine the pressures that are brought on you by lobbyists, by everybody and his brother." "Pressures?" his friend asked, "but where were your inner braces?"

The Transforming Power of a Virile Faith

Actually, the certain cure for worry is a vital, virile, Christ-centered faith, without which all other therapies fall flat in failure. It is at the point of faith that many falter, either from misunderstanding Christian faith, or, after applying it, concluding that it didn't work. In its contemporary definition, faith is little more than foolishness. Regarded as a tame, effete virtue, a mild application of positive thinking, it knows little of the real faith which Jesus taught and demonstrated.

There are individuals and groups who claim for faith things that it doesn't claim for itself. Made to fit into a round hole, this foursquare virtue is shorn of its life-transforming abilities. Not contradicting understanding, faith walks along with reason as far as reason can go. But when reason comes to the end of its road, faith is merely getting its second wind. The lament heard on every hand is "we need more faith." Actually the need is not for so much *more* faith, but for the will power to use what faith we already possess. Especially is this true since so small a pinch, like a tiny colony of atoms, when rightly activated can move mountains. When the New Testament refers to faith in action, it speaks of explosive power akin to dynamite. Faith and belief are wrapped in one indissoluble unit. When deployed, faith doesn't know what it cannot do.

Upon close self-examination, it is easy to regard one's faith as inadequate, meager, and without purposeful strength. The next step is to downgrade oneself, sometimes to the point of desperation. At this low juncture, the religious person will chart a frantic course to "get more faith" or "pray for faith." Preoccupation about faith as a thing in itself is a sort of idolatry: putting a relative virtue in the place that God should occupy. Faith in itself is nothing; however noble the virtue may be, it is like adding another zero to many zeros without an integer before them. The result still is nothing. Faith accomplishes nothing in itself; God accomplishes His purpose through active channels of intelligent faith.

Applied Faith as an Antidote to Worry

Lloyds of London, an international insurance group, will chance, through insurance with clients, that the disaster they are worrying about will never occur. Shall the world of business outdo the Christian world in its qualitative attitude toward the future course of events?

Actually, in the light of God's promises, worry is absurd. The very things over which most people worry are the same things Jesus warned against. Trusting the Word of God would come as close to being a panacea for our troubles as any existent force. Promising to supply all our need, He has gone on record to back up that promise. To cover the physical needs He has strewn earth with fruits, vegetables, nuts, fibres—a granary of plenty. Notwithstanding man's selfish monopolies and cartels whereby millions suffer privations, hunger and death, God has put enough on earth for everyone.

But the condition on which God opens the floodgate of prosperity involves one's sense of priorities. Seeking first the Kingdom of God and His kind of righteousness is prerequisite to having the secondary things added to one's account. Not that God lowers a suit of clothes or a banquet feast on a heavenly elevator; He does something better. The ripe peaches are on the low limbs in easy reach, but the tree must be planted, fertilized, sprayed and pruned. This is man's part and God has never been known to do a man's spraying for him. The Bible is replete with statements on God's end of the bargain: "My God shall supply all your need according to his riches in glory through Christ Jesus." "Cast thy burden upon the Lord for he careth for you." "And the righteous shall be like a tree planted by the rivers of water . . . and whatsoever he doeth shall prosper." "Never have I seen the righteous begging bread."

Viewed in the light of these statements, then the prayers of petition should be little more than soul-conditioning to receive what God already knows is needed. Try praying and worrying at the same time! These antithetical processes mock the name to which the prayer is directed. Trying to alleviate the burden of worrying by faithful praying is wasted effort if in the process the one praying insists on calling the plays, directing God's answer like an overzealous coach. Usually God can work it out with less interference from us. Maybe some of us ministers are guilty when it comes to telling God what the world needs, outlining in minute detail the nature of the answer that is most desired.

Few answers to prayer are as spectacular as the one that came to a chaplain friend in the Pacific in the early 1940's. His heavy bomber was forced to land on a long, white strand of beach, due to lack of gasoline. After riding the big plane to a comfortable landing, the crew became obsessed with fear that the tiny Pacific island might be occupied by enemy troops. A master sergeant put the chaplain squarely on the spot by asking, "Padre, why don't you ask your God to send us a way out of here?" The chaplain did exactly that; he prayed all afternoon that a way would be provided by which the men could escape with or without their big, expensive plane. Little did the chaplain or the other men know that some few miles away an American tanker was being trailed by a Japanese submarine and for fear of being torpedoed, the captain of the tanker had discharged raft after raft on which were strapped barrels of high octane gasoline. One of these rafts washed ashore a short distance down the beach from the grounded plane. Incredible? Not at all. The ways and means at God's disposal to accomplish what He desires defy the wildest imagination.

64

DIVINE PROVISION FOR MAN'S EMOTIONAL NEEDS

While the body must be fed, housed and clothed, these are not man's deepest needs. The heart cries out for satiation; the mind must be fed with some palatable diet; the emotions need caressing and affectionate securities. Anguish, the hunger for love, companionship in a cruel, impersonal society—all these keep recurring in the province of needs. And God has ample resources to accommodate every one of them. The "how," "when," "where," and "if" should be left to His department. Ours is the role of applied trust, unhampered mind and untrammeled soul. Herein faith has a chance to let God take the initiative.

"But aren't you afraid to live way out there in the country at your age?" an elderly, devout woman was asked. "No," she answered, "you see it is like this: faith closes the door at night; mercy opens it in the morning." Such is the glory of a human life that risks all its chances with the God who made it.

Said the Robin to the Sparrow:
"I should really like to know,
Why these anxious human beings,
Rush about and worry so!"

Said the Sparrow to the Robin:
"Friend, I think that it must be
That they have no heavenly Father,
Such as cares for you and me."[1]

[1] Elizabeth Cheney, "Overheard in an Orchard."

Life
at the
Breaking
Point

3

SALTY WATER CUT into our faces like a knife blade. Winds swirled over Luzon Harbor at thirty miles an hour, causing the troop ships to bob up and down like corks. "Overboard and up the rope ladder to the APA," the muffled orders rang out clearly in the dark, murky night. Our little party of two dozen men, weighted with nearly a hundred pounds of military gear, scurried from the small craft up the side of a large transport carrier to begin another beach landing. This time: Okinawa and Iwo Jima. Time: Easter morning.

The wet, gnarled rope ladder, no wider than a man's body, kept swaying away from the ship. Bouncing back to the steel side as the transport wallowed from port to starboard, the rope ladder presented an awesome challenge. My close friend, a dental officer, was two rungs up the ladder ahead of me when I heard him say that he could not hold on any longer. The unaccustomed weight, the wet, frightening, cruel weather, but mostly swinging out from the ship sometimes fifteen feet, to be followed by a dull, painful thud as his body would be pounded against the ship, had exhausted him. "But, you've got to go on up there," I shouted. "Think of your wife and three daughters. Don't turn loose now!" "But I can't hold out another minute," he cursingly shouted as blood dripped from the grip of his hands. "Then for God's sake if you can't hold out, hold on!" I shouted back. He took a firmer grip, gritted his teeth, and with one final stroke of effort, climbed over onto the deck.

Sooner or later most people will come to the low moments when life's climb gets too steep and the load too heavy to carry. Their burdens increase in tonnage while muscles for carrying sag and tire. The nature of things is such that if one lives a normal span of years, getting involved is a usual routine. This fact assures one that his pathway will lead him into some dark valleys where the powers of death and darkness lurk. Unwariness is hardly effective armor for this eventuality.

Last week a man recited a long decalogue of debts he owed, domestic troubles that marred his married life, along with the dim prospect of things being otherwise in the future. Said he, "Preacher, I have to look up even to see the bottom." His name is legion; millions are enmeshed in a tangle of seemingly hopeless webs and have about convinced themselves that there is no way out. This is a tragic spectacle; like an animal cornered, cowed and cringing, the person fights back with ineffectual effort, often preferring ever-narrowing angles of the corner to an all-out effort to escape the corner.

The fact of coming close to life's breaking point now and then is not the gravest concern. Maintaining awareness of the extreme danger as well as activating enough willpower to pull away from the breaking point is the most pronounced issue involved.

An ever-growing fraternity of fatalists compound this low estate of despair, despondency and defeatism. These disciples of defeatism not only stifle any initiative but swear that the bottom is the normal habitat. Their theme song echoes, "Cheer up, the worst is ahead." Every roseate pronouncement that things are not as bad as they seem, or that as long as there is life there is hope, is rebuffed by a cynical snarl of vulgar impiety. Quite logically, an attitude that gives no quarter to perspective or optimism rooted in Christian faith will lead to fatalism almost every time.

These are the discordant prophets who contend that man is "a sick fly on the wheel of fate," or who say with Darrow that, "Life is an unpleasant interruption of nothingness." Listen to the funeral dirge in the mouth of Macbeth,

> . . . it [life] is a tale
> Told by an idiot, full of sound and fury,
> Signifying nothing.[1]

In The Rubaiyat of Omar Khayyam, the prober for substance and essence beyond the temporal sphere concludes:

> I sent my Soul through the invisible,
> Some letter of that after-life to spell:
> And by and by my Soul return'd to me
> And answered "I Myself am Heav'n and Hell."[2]

Desperate individuals who stand on tiptoe on the brink of the breaking point are quick to point out the fiascoes of nature, the exceptions that prove the rule, focusing on the inexplicable mysteries of life. Any Christian is equally honest in admitting these; but while he is not able to solve the deeper mysteries, he knows the One who can. One informed fatalist countered my contention that heroic service and sacrifice in a noble cause bigger than ourselves is a worthy goal by relating the story of the "unnecessary" death of George Borup. Borup, one of Commodore Peary's men in the expedition to the North Pole, was known for his prowess as a swimmer. Crossing icy crevasses, falling into floes which would have been a frigid tomb to weaker men, George managed to wrest himself free. Upon returning home from that thrilling adventure, he was drowned in a farm pond only two acres in size! The contrast does look like something of a comedy of errors. Yes, the worst attitude possible for us when we come to the deep shadows and want to give up is to let fatalism creep in and install itself as the captain of the team who calls all the plays.

Did anyone ever encounter such an adverse chain of ill circumstances as that Old Testament character, Job? Read and interpret it as you may, the basic fact is not altered: if any mortal in history had legitimate grounds for wanting to throw in the sponge, it was Job. Provoked into complaints about God, his peeve did not become a renunciation of God. True, he repudiated his old faith;

[1] William Shakespeare, *Macbeth*, Act V, Sc. 3, Line 19.
[2] Omar Khayyam, *Rubaiyat*, Stanza 66. Translated by Edward Fitzgerald.

but this was part of the providential purpose in permitting the boils, poverty, family demise and the unholy surrounding of "friends" whose presence defeated their pale intentions. The act of repudiating his old faith was the process in which new faith was born.

"Curse God and die," his wife said in monotonous, pagan disgust. Yet, my efforts to castigate this woman leave me cold and mute; maybe she wasn't nearly so sacrilegious as she was sincere. With every vestige of God's visible evidence gone, not a trace that He either knew or cared remaining, perhaps her cry was a lamentation against the whole, horrible scheme of things. Maybe she took it as long as she could; then her love for Job wouldn't permit visible witnessing of that insufferable lot any longer.

His answer is like a fresh wind that blows through a stuffy building. "Thou foolish woman. . . ." That says enough in itself! Foolishness indicates that wisdom has taken its leave of a person and only folly remains within. "Have we not received good and evil at God's hand?" Job asked her. Run an average through your days, months and years. Add the prosperous seasons when life was a lark, when everything seemed to move in your direction, when the lights all turned green just for you. When you are honest enough to add the assets along with the liabilities, the picture changes. This regimen will offset many a night of dismay, horror and distraction.

Today we are beset with more dramatic visitations than those of Job. Hurts inflicted from unknown enemies in ambush, unexplained evil in high places, suffering of the innocent, starvation of children—these beset us in undiminished assault. Small wonder that human response often is an attitude of "I don't care," or "survival of the fittest," or "root pig or die." Giving up may add one more mound to an expanding cemetery, but it won't solve the problem of mastering the hard lot and improving it by God's blessed help.

In his book *Supposition and Certainty* George MacDonald tells of a woman who wished she had never been made. When her minister had heard the foolish complaint long enough, he rebuked

69

the woman by saying, "You haven't been made yet, woman. God is still making you and you are quarreling with his processes."

It is not fatal to fall. The only dismaying aspect of a spill is if it is repeated so often that there is no inclination left to get up. A worm is one of the few things that can't fall down. Life is like riding a bicycle: either you go on or you go off. Standing still is an impossibility. The fact that pencils still have erasers is proof that men still make mistakes. More fatalism is spawned by those who take that initial step toward God, but who fail to go on to the many other steps in the wondrous adventure of becoming like Him. That small boy epitomized this naked truth when asked by his mother why he fell out of bed the previous night. "I don't know, Mother, unless I went to sleep too near where I got in." No comfortable margin is left on life's mattress if, after entering the redemptive venture, we fall asleep too near the place where we got in.

FORCES WHICH LEAD TO THE BREAKING POINT

No rational person deliberately chooses to walk into a snake pit of despair. When life crowds one in a corner, usually there are several forces which have been at work over an extended period of time. As important as finding the right exit from the corner is finding what led to the corner in the first place. The turns in the road causing one to miss his main highway should be noted. Many times a variety of forces weld together causing one to lose heart, lose touch with reality, and to move around in a detached, disinterested way.

Many of these forces are of our own making: intemperance, bad health resulting from negligence, business catastrophes resulting from fool-hardy vanity, domestic trouble stemming from taking some of life's finest privileges for granted—these and many more. Still, it must be conceded that there is a province of events and circumstances that force persons to the point of no return, a province not caused by any fault or sin of the individual involved. The corner is there, nonetheless, with all its prisonlike restrictions.

MENTAL ILLNESS—AN ESCORT TO THE BREAKING POINT

> *The mind is its own place, and in itself*
> *Can make a heaven of hell, a hell of heaven.*[3]

This gem of wise understanding from John Milton represents man's hard-learned wisdom. "Out of the heart come the issues of life," and in this case the mind is involved. When the mind becomes sick, all phases of the personality suffer. External circumstances cause their share of trouble and vexation, but what goes on deep in the labyrinths of the human mind is far more determinative.

Mental illness stands as a foreboding spectre on the horizon of the twentieth century. Its heavy toll in human happiness and freedom is just beginning. This very hour millions would sooner be dead than living. "What's the use in it all?" This question recurs daily and sometimes hourly among those who demonstrate the death impulse in their lives. This is a type of mental illness, since life in its healthy condition essentially is an unconscious desire for continuity.

The first symptoms of mental illness should be regarded with sensible gravity and handled accordingly. It isn't good enough to say, "Oh, it's all in your mind; go forget about it." Were it that easy, many already would have forgotten about it! Obviously, this is the easily given advice of the slow of understanding. And while no quarter is to be yielded to that chasm of imaginary ills and pains, when can one be positively sure what part is real and what part is imaginary?

A thinking individual stands today amidst the shambles of creeds that have been wrecked in his own lifetime. Many of the old allegiances are as dead as a dodo. New allegiances are shabby, and many are unworthy. For instance, Sigmund Freud once was ex-

[3] John Milton, *Paradise Lost*, Book I, Line 253.

alted as the ultimate answer to human needs and expressions. Multithousands not only saw in his words and findings the answer to the human problem, but made of his findings a complete way of life. Today, more balanced findings prove how fragmentary Freud was, after all. Most analysts, including many who formerly genuflected before Freud's psychoanalytical altars, now have all but rejected his efforts to reduce man to "a problem of instinctual mechanics."

GUILT AND MENTAL ILLNESS

"Preacher, no matter what I do, or how long I pray, it seems that God is breathing down my neck; I have confessed all to Him, but still, I can't sleep, my medicine cabinet looks like a junior prescription counter and, frankly, I have lost interest in my job, my wife, and about everything else. Everything, that is, but God." I noticed that the last mentioned was tacked on as something of an afterthought. Then I countered by asking, "You say that you have confessed all your wrong to God; then do you feel that He has forgiven you?" "I suppose so," the hesitant answer came. "But what does that have to do with my wanting to see a psychiatrist and take shock treatment?" he kept saying. He had become so convinced that there was some magic involved in shock therapy, that he was stumbling over the real cause and cure for his condition. The thought of his guilt stopped him in the middle of a smile or a handshake.

We looked at the nature of his sin, at his sincerity in getting it out of him and trusting God through Jesus Christ to forgive him. This to him, as to me, is still incredible: how God can take our sins on Him is the wondrous, though ineffable, mystery. But for that matter, so is nearly everything God has done. What a happy thought, though, that God's creative initative does not have to wait for human understanding. Finally, my friend saw that his mental sickness was stemming from a mind that was freighted with guilt.

The right way to handle this asset-liability is to face it head on and know that two courses of action are open to any person. If one's guilt is the result of intentional sins—sins that have not been confessed—then the only intelligent action is confession, repentance, and changed behavior. If guilt is imaginary, self-imposed either by unexplained martyrdom or desire to be hurt—one of the tragic angles of mental illness—then the right course of action is to absolve the guilt by sensible thinking and firmness of will power, both of which can come as helps from God.

No constructive purpose is served by a life bowed down under a yoke of guilt's tonnage. Least of all can a Christian be a winning witness when guilt is wrongly present. "You can bear anything if it isn't your own fault," some one has aptly observed.

NEGATIVE AVENUES OF ESCAPE FROM LIFE'S BREAKING POINTS

It is essential to know what roads not to take out of death's valley. Many problems are made more difficult by desperate attempts at every sort of solution. Running down every one-way street because of frantic pressure to get out of the corner digs the rut in the road deeper rather than lifting one out of it. Herein the cure is worse than the disease.

Millions are trying to escape the anxieties spawned by a world of contradictions. To what extent the inordinate emphasis on space exploration figure in man's desperate efforts to escape the reality of this earth is interesting speculation. Trying to reconcile sane optimism with honest pessimism presents a precarious challenge, much like trying to walk a tight rope. Many people are convinced that the direction out of this morass lies in change of environment; so they move from place to place, change jobs, covet greener fields, but in the process they intensify the civil war within. No, the answer isn't geography. Where a person lives and works is hardly the real issue; who he is matters primarily. This business of life is a battle in which we fall from wounds received in running away. Place and proximity seldom determine either happiness or unhappiness. Not the outer areas, but man's internal assets—his calibre of soul-fibre, his posture in morals, his sensitivity—these are the potential plateaus or sloughs of despondency. Within this inner citadel of man's personality reside unsightly, negative faculties. Therein man finds an unbuttressed, unversed self whose softness is at odds with the rigors of intellectual self-discipline.

When one is standing in the bottom of the pit is no time to hear, "I told you so," or "If you had done this, that, or the other, you wouldn't be in this predicament." No one knows the truth of that unconsoling verdict better than the one at the near-breaking point. Few preachments are more cruel than those severe, though truthful, words that cut straight into the open wound of mental anguish and acute anxiety. Through bloodshot eyes, with a haggard expression, the prisoner of emotions looks up at this "telling off" with chagrin, hurt, wounded pride and disgust. But he can ill afford any of these sentiments when he stands at the razor-edge of death.

The Negative Road of Functional Atheism

There are many ways of saying that there is no God. Few indeed say it overtly as was once the case. Who hears of an atheist nowadays renting the local municipal auditorium in order to give his lecture on why he does not believe in God? But not many decades ago this was a fairly common practice. Is it that our generation is more devout than preceding generations? Hardly. Part of the answer lies in the fact that they possessed a firmer courage and a brasher vocality than present-day atheists. Some individuals arrived at their atheistic position in an "honest" way. That is, they searched the annals of religious lore, traveled, argued in defense of religion, witnessed the panorama of religious spectacle and human cruelties. They took the sophomoric, survey courses in religion while in college, which exposed them to a few of the surface issues without thoroughly going into any of them. When their courses in biology, geology or anthropology claimed one position of man's origin and growth while much of what they heard in the field of religion and humanities "contradicted" the conclusions in the natural sciences, they forsook the latter. It was at this point that such a student felt that he had to make his choice—a choice between what he deemed sensible logic and mythological nonsense called religion. When a student arrives at this juncture by laborious effort—as sterile and erroneous as it is—still he deserves an edge over one who never wrestles with the deep things of life. The latter type seldom if ever asks: "Who am I?" "From where did I come?" "What am I here for?" and more important, "Who is back of all this?" This type of atheist goes ahead and organizes his life as though there were no God. At best, if there is a God, He is so far removed from human events, so ethereal and detached, that it is the height of folly to presume such a one would pay any attention to something so finite as a human being. With that agnostic conclusion, life is one series of blunders after another.

"God is dead," if one listens to French philosopher Jean Paul Sartre. This state of mental sterility according to Sartre leaves "man alone, abandoned on earth in the midst of his finite responsibilities." During the postwar period Sartre's despair-filled "existentialist" philosophy appealed to that frame of mind which sought some bridge to span the world that died at Pearl Harbor and the world being born in the decade thereafter. Today, this offbeat way of thinking, like other novelties which have no ground in divine reality, has faded.

Ignoring God is the worst kind of folly. This is to resign oneself to the half life of a coward. The functional atheist exercises more deadening influence than his more vocal predecessor. At least the former type of atheist did not veil his vacuum-life; he even boasted of his emptiness.

Life organized around the center of human ego is a sorry structure. Either relegating God to the outer rim or according Him no place at all is atheism in lethal form.

One such God-denying man paraphrased the prayer Jesus taught His disciples to pray:

Our Brethren, who are upon the earth;
Hallowed by our name. Our kingdom come, our will be done
On earth for there is no heaven.

We must get this day our daily bread,
We neither forgive nor are forgiven.

Let us be led into temptation
Since deliverance from evil is no fun anyway.

For ours is the kingdom, ours the power, and ours the glory,
And there is no forever and forever!

The peculiar danger of standing low in the valley of despair is the temptation to sour on God. Souring is easy, since there are so many sour personality patterns around. This condition is more contagious than the itch. In the grip of sourness, prayer seems to be wasted words. Nearly every desperate soul who is at the brink of personality disintegration will quickly tell you that no matter how often or how long he prays, he feels that God hears nothing, or if He does, He says nothing by way of heeding the petition. Worse still, he knows of a certainty that He is forever remote—too remote for him to feel any sense of His nearness. One rational minute would reveal an elemental, basic fact about God's nature: He is omnipresent, whether one feels as if He is or not. What does it matter how one feels about God? Emotions are not the only track on which He can travel to the inner citadel of the soul.

There is no substitute for a qualitative trust in God's nearness. To believe that He will set the record straight, that He does care, that His nature is love in action is requisite to getting out of the snake pit. God will put all your stars back in the sky, if you will let Him. When life's circumstances get too hot to handle, let them go—into the hands of God!

The Negative Road of Self-Destruction
Suicide: The Final Stroke of Desperation

> *"Would I were dead, were God's*
> *good will so,*
> *For what is life but grief and woe?"*
> —*Shakespeare*

The Pentagon was stunned, the Armed Forces dismayed, and the nation shocked when the daily newspaper May 22, 1949 read: "DEFENSE SECRETARY JAMES FORRESTAL IS DEAD." A few lines of reading revealed the startling facts that this well-informed,

dedicated man had plunged to his death from the sixteenth floor
of Bethesda Naval Hospital. Shortly before he took his life, he
copied from an old volume the disenchanting words of Sophocles:

> When Reason's Day
> Sets rayless—joyless—quenched in cold decay,
> Better to die, and sleep
> The never waking sleep, than linger on
> And dare to live, when the soul's life is gone.

One can never know how many small streams flow together making the river that consumes life. That there are many tributary
causes, rather than a single factor, is admissible, scientific truth.
The consensus that the will to live is the strongest force within
human make-up is ill based in fact. In some individuals the death
impulse outweighs the will to live from the cradle to the grave. I
have fought on the field of battle with men who not only wanted
to die, but actually registered disappointment when their efforts
to get killed were not successful. Some physicians agree that control and utilization of this destructive force is the number one
problem of modern mankind.

When a person finally feels that every means of escape or solution has been tried and has failed, then the chilling conclusion
creeps in: life has completely forsaken him, no friends are left, no
one understands his predicament. Close on the heels of this obsession is the question: Then why keep on trying? Then the mind
flushes with a psychotic lilt as the idea of self-destruction enters.
To be out of it! What a step forward that would be! So he reasons.

Most people have had some such thoughts whether consciously
or by indirect, subconscious desire. Not that they actually thought
of taking their lives, but vicariously they drank the poison or pulled
the trigger, exploring by imagination what the experience would
be like. Of course, it took but a few seconds to snap back to the
bridge of normalcy and forget it. That such ideas flash through your
mind is no cause for alarm, any more than one should be alarmed
by the parade of other equally imaginary, erroneous ideas. It is
noteworthy that the only times such thoughts appear to normal,

healthy people is during duress, fatigue or lost direction. Sooner or later most people will come to that point of Hamlet's dilemma, "To be or not to be: that is the question." Is it worthwhile to keep on bucking the sea of life with its tempestuous waves, or is it better to give in to the sea and die?

Each year in America 16,000 men and women take their own lives. This figure represents twice the number of murders. Experts in law enforcement agencies, psychiatrists, ministers and social workers estimate that another 100,000 men and women attempt suicide each year but do not succeed. Every thirty-three minutes another life destroys itself in our nation alone. For every woman who kills herself, three men commit suicide, though three times as many women attempt self-destruction as men. Police records of one major city show 300 attempts of suicide by women in a given period. Less than a dozen of these were fatal. In a six-months period recently, four people plunged to their death from the eighty-sixth floor of New York's Empire State building. Sixteen people have been known to jump from that perch. What it is about height that lures the person who is death-bent on destroying himself is still a mystery. Part of the answer lies in the inexpensive, guaranteed finality. Part of it is a desire to go out spectacularly, even if the poor, demented soul enjoyed nothing spectacular while living.

One would think from the morbid nature of the facts that most suicides would occur at a certain time of the year—probably in the cold, bleak, drabness of winter when the spirit is apt to draw itself in. But the months of May and June claim the highest number of those who exit from life by their own hands. Mondays and Tuesdays walk off with the highest record—far more so than weekends. Bad weather apparently is no factor, since fine weather witnesses more use of poison, pistols and plunges than foul weather. Yet these facts imply logical reasoning and we are talking about irrational, illogical behavior.

The Human Mind: Source of Self-Destruction Impulses

The human brain, like the human heart, represents more complexity, resiliency, power, and mystery than any other single entity. The brain must perform all the functions for the body in the way of command; the mystery is not that so many can be impaired by a combination of forces, but that so comparatively few are impaired. A wonderful, precise mechanism is the brain. This fact is reason enough to cultivate it and care for it. Decisions are made that determine one's longevity, his happiness, and whether or not a berserk mind will wreak havoc in the world—all within the brain.

A quick glance at its anatomy reveals three general areas. First, the conscious self. In this region occur thought and decision involving human action and interaction. Second, there is the preconscious, where memories and thoughts are stored. This division is the library of the mind, capable of storing all the facts in the twelve million volumes in the Library of Congress. Herein are the memories of childhood, thoughts memorized, experiences recorded. The difficulty of recalling names, for instance, merely indicates a poor filing system of the mind's library shelves—nothing wrong with the shelves or the names.

The third section, the subconscious self, is the one that is most difficult to understand. In a sense it is the basement of the mind. The finest furniture is not placed in a mansion's basement but in the drawing rooms. And like the dwelling, the subconscious mind catches all the unsightly wrappings and trappings of life's activities. Here irrational thoughts reside; here the so-called "crazy" dreams lurk.

When certain activities are sublimated or suppressed, this activity is little more than packing down in the basement of the subconscious mind unrealized desires or vicarious experiences. Much of life's daydreaming reflects the residue of the mind's basement. Old angers, resentments, and inequities have a way of descending to the subconscious mind only to come back up at the most inopportune time, as well as in the most embarrassing ways. Here is the locale of sexual aberrations which occur at cross purposes with the conscious mind, thereby setting up all types of tension and frustration. If one could look in this dimly lit area, the sight would reveal all sorts of lusty thoughts, malignant anxieties, wrath, unexpressed appetites, wounded feelings, erratic wishes, etc. Needless to add that the fire hazard of the personality is in this "basement." From it come neuroses, psychoses, and sometimes insanity.

So long as a person is in command of his wits, so long as he rules the kingdom of his personality from conscious choice, just so long is he considered sane. It is when the personality takes up residence in the basement, when he describes the world from that underground outlook, that his conduct, thought and will take a psychotic direction. Life gets closer and closer to the breaking point, as personality moves into the basement altogether, where contact with reality is severed. The death impulses enter at that point—impulses of self-destruction.

Forms of Suicide

Now that we have seen a sketchy portrait of mental make-up, let us look at some forms of self-destruction. They are more manifold and varied than the average person would think. Is it possible for a sane person to take his own life? That question is asked each time a suicide is reported. When life turns on itself and desires death above life, when every overture to rational thinking is rebuffed by an overpowering death impulse, what is a person to do? How is he to be helped? Not every suicide is an act of cowardice; it may be one of courage. At least a courage of sorts, for had he been able to live with defection, he would have been no man at all. But the enormity of his crime was such that his sensitive soul could not live up to its realization.

Then there are some men and women who take their lives without having any morbid longing for death. They become disappointed in love, or business, or other involvements, and during a low cycle of emotional down-drafts and unreasoned fury, life is snuffed out. Sloughs of self-pity, quagmires of depression, swamps of resentment which so easily can be the incubators of the death-dealing activity, all figure in some case histories of self-annihilation.

Chronic-Lineal Suicide

Sudden, violent destruction of life is but one way to kill. For every one who shoots or poisons himself, there are uncounted multitudes who slowly take their own lives. This is a type of chronic, sustained self-murder. The differences are twofold: the technique is more subtle and less gory while the time element is more drawn out. Life is subjected to the slow death which may take years to complete. This effort is designed to bring life to a standstill by putting to death the will to live, by resisting all overtures which aim at improving man's sorry lot. Such negation springs from man's most primitive beginnings where desire for progress was nearly nonexistent. The chronic suicide registers not a flicker of interest in any force which would propel him forward.

In this group are the men and women who lack the courage to end life all at once, but also lack the heart to make something out of the circumstances from which they would remove themselves—hence the contradiction. Usually there is just enough interest in the biological necessities to prevent starvation or total prostration. Moving about like zombies, people like this never hear the voices that would help them snap out of it. So the decision is made: gradual self-extinction.

It is a bit ironical that many such folk are regularly found in church. Theirs is not the motive of intelligent worship, or of seeking divine guidance to live a life of purposeful positiveness. Rather, they come, sit, stare, gaze, and "enjoy" the whole show by virtue of the unconscious inner defiance and rebellion to much that is seen, done and heard in church. Since the person plans no future, then all talk about faith, immortality, hope and courage belong to the vernacular of others, not to the self-destroyer. This negative euphoria, this enjoyment in reverse, speaks of a sick mind where logic and reason are inverted. All efforts to elevate, heal, love or direct one who has permitted the cement of his mind to set are met with the same "no comment." As fatal as poison is this escape hatch of life.

Self-Punishment a Kind of Suicide

Dr. Arnold Hutschnecker in his book *The Will To Live* concludes, "Man dies when he wants to die." Such a statement on first reading sounds awry of the truth. Especially to those who have witnessed that monolithic struggle when death knocks at life's door and every force within the sick patient votes "no." At such times full alarm is sounded throughout the body, summoning every soldier of vein, nerve and muscle to live! But the fact remains that the illusive, strange thing called "life" can be manipulated to a great extent at will. For instance, a person carrying around twenty to thirty pounds of extra weight knows that he is digging his grave with his teeth. The excess pounds mean that the heart will pound unnecessarily and every chore is made more difficult. This is a type of suicide, though fortunately most obese people are not purposive suicides. They are just compulsive eaters.

When a person hates another, whether it is his wife, parent or competitor, the desire to kill, to destroy is inherent in the hate. But the horrendous thought of actually killing is forthrightly banished from his mind. Casting out the idea of murder leaves a cavity of guilt which begins its corrosive processes in the subconscious. Feeling that some time must be served because of the murder which he wanted to commit and knowing that no person, court, jury or judge even knows about the intentional murder, logic suggests that he must be judge, jury and jail. Not giving himself too much benefit of the doubt, he then passes sentence and begins serving time by self-punishment. Denying himself many legitimate things and activities, his only feeling of emotional security comes with the process of denial. He is convinced that he is guilty and guilt must be atoned by self-imprisonment.

Fragments of Scripture along with erroneous interpretations of the fragments endorse this desperate person's decision to punish and chastise. A negative outlook on life is always characteristic of the chronic suicide. Bright skies, lovely flowers and soul-stirring music leave him cold and unmoved.

In less charitable phraseology, the name is kill-joy. Since he is serving an internal prison term, then anything that would produce levity and pleasure is off limits. Few of this type will become zealous about anyone else enjoying life. While the person knows that his decision to punish himself is his own, inadvertently he resents a good time for others: another of the contradictory aspects of the predicament.

Incapacity for enjoying anything becomes more pronounced. In the context of love and marriage, sex to this sort usually is other than wholesome. A thousand-and-one mental reservations arise to haunt, hound and slow the initiative in sexual love. The emotional life is taken out of circulation as affections are reined and put in deep-freeze. The normal capacities for sex, warmth and affection are allowed to fade away by default and desire. Auxiliary to the guilt factor in this connection are puritanical teachings, prudish mores, ignorance, sadism, selfishness and a host of undesirable facets that prod guilt on its dastardly way. The results: frigidity and impotence. Guilt does its lethal work well. For all practical purposes, the body is held in a state of functional paralysis.

After a quarter of a century of counseling, my files are filled with case after case where the warm springs of affection and love dried up because of self-punishment activated by a pathological sense of overriding guilt.

These are the less dramatic type of self-murderers, illustrated by a young doctor who, in a fit of anger, murdered his only child. Committed to an asylum for the insane, he felt a sigh of relief when finally the key turned in the lock to confine him. Then time rolled by and his mind fixed on his guilt and what he must do for atonement. A few days later, he purposely thrust his right arm into the huge propellers of a washing machine. The arm was mangled beyond repair, but within a few days he returned to a type of clear sanity after feeling that he had done some sort of penance for murdering his child. The self-mutilation was his way of taking at least a part of his own life in an act of atonement.

Intentional Accidents

When for no apparent reason a person swerves his car into the path of an approaching vehicle or over an embankment, many times it can be concluded that death was the intention of the driver. For a brief time, the compulsion to end it all dominated the mind.

Aquatic experts insisted that Hope Root, a Miami attorney, who descended into sea depths off Florida, was "suicidal" when he insisted upon wearing the weights strapped to his waist instead of holding them in his hands for easy release. Daredevil chances taken by hot-rod drivers, aerialists, and in other sports frequently reflect this courting of death. Said the Marquis De Portago, just before he was killed while racing his car, "I prefer the lightning speed because death seems closer every moment." How else is one to explain a middle-aged man deliberately walking out in front of a moving vehicle?

An Amalgam of Types

"She is back in the hospital for her fourth operation and seems as happy as a lark," a distant cousin told me as I called on a former church member. This statement revived in my memory the doctor's reaction to her former operations. His patient demanded surgery. When no alternative suggestion worked, he consented to the minor operation largely out of a desire to help the patient's attitude. This "knife-happy" patient is another type in the long list of those who set themselves to the infamous business of self-extinction. Removing one part of the body is at least another step toward removing the entire body.

Self-imposed martyrdom and asceticism constitute functional suicide. Asceticism is the outlook that dogmatically contends that anything which makes for merriment and joy somehow must belong to evil—activities producing recreational fun are the work of Satan and therefore should be shunned as one would shun a rattlesnake. What preposterous misrepresentation of facts! The Church of Jesus Christ is never so misunderstood as when Jesus is portrayed as a negator who wanders through life with a long face, desiring death. He does no such thing! His was an infectious life of regnant joy, living with all the stops pulled out; not as a sinful libertine, but as one who knew that to the pure all things are pure. No, not a libertine, but one who had been set free by Almighty God.

The long-faced, sackcloth-and-ashes type of religionist does more harm to genuine Christian faith than ever can be measured. Always tired and negative, such a person becomes bored and boring. A veritable volcano of petty strifes, he thrives on crises in the household of faith. In the words of an eminent psychiatrist when refer-

84

ring to a patient who saw everything and everybody as evil, "She was an injustice collector."

The site of life's breaking points is no holy ground. Nor is it a place where one should tarry, lest it become his final piece of ground—a grave! The pit of a well is a poor place from which to judge the human race.

Chapter IV points out the alternatives to such futility—the positive avenues of exodus from the valley of defeat, the roads leading out of the dark!

The Way Out of the Dark

4

"To look around is to be distressed. To look within is to be depressed. To look up is to be blessed."—Raymond Becker

"Commit thy way unto the Lord . . . He shall direct thy paths . . ."— Psalm 37:5, Proverbs 3:6

IN THE FOREGOING chapter a dark picture of desperation, frantic bewilderment and self-destruction left unanswered the central question: Is there a way out of the darkness? A door of hope from the breaking point? The answer is a happy affirmative: Yes, there is a road out of the dark—a positive, straight road leading to good health, and intelligent significance. To imply that the road is easily traveled is far from the truth or from my intention. Nothing in life worth possessing is easily obtained, least of all that secure ground on which one can stand when struggling free from the low terrain near the breaking point.

The titanic tragedy involved in such dire circumstance is the loss of faith, without which man will not struggle on. The hope for our kind is not to forego anxiety but to endure it triumphantly. Running from life's battles will guarantee nothing more than additional chances for cowardice. When faith is but a puny, tender plant in human personality, anxiety will become a rugged, virile weed. In passionate pursuit of materialism, we have sacrificed the one force which we could least afford to lose: a virile faith that holds together the loose components of life. Our hope is not in slower pace, less noise, reduced numbers, more money, or longevity, Few of these are apt to contribute much.

There is no magic that will do the trick for our modern malady. Yet, such magic is what millions want and sometimes demand.

86

Some pill, some right mixture of chemicals, some panacea which will dismiss the load of guilt, fears, neuroses and negative thinking. The way out of the dark begins with the admission that peace must be made on the inside—deep inside the human soul—where it really counts. In no other way can tension be made man's servant rather than his master. The negative margins of human experience are converted into positive assets when the individual ceases to be a walking civil war. The foul streams of self-mutilation and suffering then can be drained off into channels that will not pollute or defile either self or others. When the internal walls of the mind and soul are cleansed, no longer then will guilt cry out, "Macbeth shall sleep no more."

ALTERNATIVES TO FUTILITY

The Role of the Individual

Part of the initiative in an about-face from the brink of disaster must come from the individual involved. Another portion of the process must be the initiative of other people. The greater portion belongs to the loving, caring heart of God. With this trio in mind, the hapless struggler can first analyze his position, take stock and see how close he stands to the precipitous cliff—then the road back up isn't as steep as it looks to be. One thing in the desperate person's favor is the presence of so many other people at the edge of doom. While this doesn't move him one inch from his individual threat, it should engender new heart in knowing that his is not a unique predicament. A veritable community of sufferers is somewhere near that extreme depot where the bottom is more familiar than any other place on life's incline. But to feel that one is all alone will both shove him further down and discourage any personal effort to climb out and up. One must take honest stock of his whole life when he thinks the jig is up. A visitor to Atlanta's Fox Theatre during Metropolitan Opera Week last year mistook the intermission for the end of the program, and began commenting on the quality of the opera while getting his hat and coat to go home. The last half of the program, even with the grande finale, could hardly relieve

87

the man's embarrassment. No, life isn't necessarily over just because the curtain closes momentarily. It may be just the intermission. Hanging on one more minute may be the difference between life and death.

The Penetrating Question: Is Life Really Worth Living?

Once an individual has taken honest inventory, surveyed the dimension of his problems, then he is in line for answering a summary question: "Is life really worth living?" The answer he gives to this question will determine whether or not he continues to live.

Asking the question, "Is life worth living?" raises a resounding "Yes" from multitudes of people. Many of these have discovered the scarlet thread of purpose in life. Theirs is more than creature comfort or animal existence. But other multitudes honestly reply to this question, "No, life isn't worth the effort to live." These are the folks who have discovered the purpose many times, but have refused to fit into it or follow its call. Others, after reasonable, honest and diligent search, have found nothing but a predominance of contradiction, misery and fatalism. One need not be classed as a pagan when admitting that life can be a sorry affair; this fact is seen, not only in the inevitable approach of old age and death, but also seen in struggle, disease, debts, disappointments, and frustrating tensions.

This universe, instead of being an orderly cosmos, often is a cruelly impersonal chaos, wreaking havoc through lashing earthquakes, pestilence, wind, fire and flood. Disease, knowing no respectability of "off limits" to saints, rudely invades all manner of men, cutting them down with its insatiable scythe. Corporate evil, with double fists, rides the earth in brute force, leaving in its wake the agonizing groans of innocent millions. The mills of the gods are grinding entirely too slowly to provide enough grist for human consumption.

Yes, life can be one hectic crisis after another, leaving the soul out of breath. It also can be a thrilling privilege, a wondrous adventure through uncharted scenery, where one may experience new di-

88

mension, new latitude in enjoyment and appreciation. Every such exhilarating experience suggests an additional one until, like an excursion through magic gardens, life becomes an increasing rapture.

Is such living really possible, or is such talk little more than verbal embroidery to spread over the hard, cold facts of brutality, boredom and bestiality?

Life Is Worth Living so Long as There Is Wrong To Be Righted

Jesus clearly stated that the kind of life He came to impart was abundant—that is, full to overflowing, not with filler but with genuine content. His sort of abundance tilts the days toward the sunshine of significance. His kind of life is zestful, charged with the magnetism of otherness and onwardness. His teachings are replete with verbs—words of action, words of militant decisiveness. So long as evil is on the throne and right on the scaffold, then just so long is life a challenge to those who would fight in order to set the record straight. Such corrective involvement is the hardest kind of fighting, since the opposition of evil must not resort to evil methods. The thing that is wrong must be attacked without wrathful belligerence. In a word, one must hate sin and love the sinner without confusing the two. The admonition, "Be angry and sin not," still is in the Bible and continues to be relevant. There is such a thing as holy anger, but it is possible only among those who have matured in the grace of Christlike submission. Otherwise, one is surely rationalizing while exercising a temper which may equal or exceed the evil that he is attacking.

The truest index of a man is that which measures him by his resistance to evil. Measure him in terms of cash if you will, and you have nothing more than a bank account. If in terms of prestige you place him on the rule, you read from it little more than an aggregate of human opinion. Measure him in terms of years and you have only chronologies of days and years. By the standards of the world one may be measured to little permanent avail, but measure a man in the quality of his resistence to tyranny and you find a man indeed.

Once to every man and nation comes the moment to decide;
In the strife of Truth with falsehood, for the good or evil side;
Some great cause, God's new Messiah, offering each the bloom or blight,

* * *

And the choice goes by forever 'twixt that darkness and that light.[1]

Life Is Worth Living so Long as There Is Gloom To Be Chased

As the wheel of human experience continues its inexorable journey, the cycles of elation and gloom cut their grooves more deeply with each revolution. Unless one's guard stays up, the cycles of gloom will recur with greater frequency than the cycles of delight and elation. One of society's greatest needs is gloom-chasers, those rare souls who are willing not only to demonstrate real quality in their own lives, but who go out of their way to brighten the lives of others. They refuse membership in that fraternity of fatalists who refuse to extend a helping hand or a loving embrace to the man or woman standing close to the danger line.

Gloom and despair, like a gritty whirlwind, descend upon us, filling the eyes of the soul with obscuring particles. These death-dealing forces enter lives with demanding severity. So long as we prate about morals and mental health while giving ourselves to materialism, just so long will the world's ill go unhealed.

A keyed-up, hypertensive type of person is a perennial candidate for gloom, since he insists that life forever be in high gear. Riding the escalator of one high peak after another without the essential, restorative valleys in between is his constant demand. Like Elijah fleeing from the wrathful Jezebel, he flees reality while thinking that escape will present a brightness all its own. And like Elijah who chose a juniper tree to sit under and weep in self-pity, he indulges the monster within. In the process, his gloom is intensified.

Then an accommodating God grows a trailing vine up the juniper tree of self-pity to shade those doubting mortals until they return to the job where they belong. Gloom can take the pastels of life and repigment them with burnt umber and battleship gray. No wonder the Bible keeps calling man back to a triumphant attitude, a

[1] James Russell Lowell, "The Present Crisis."

90

winning disposition, a radiant smile as indices of faith and spiritual health. Nothing to live for? Indeed there is, as long as gloom needs to be driven from human experience.

Life knows a worthwhileness so long as there are tears to be dried. In this devastatingly impersonal world, tears flow with easy abandon. More and more dependence on mechanical skills and the dreams of interplanetary travel will serve to make less personal much of what the future generations will do. Already it is possible to live and die in a big, cold city while few people know anything about it or care. Under such conditions, life could be greatly enhanced if more of us made it a point to relieve, if but temporarily, some of the miseries which cause the flow of tears. Some reassuring word, some kind gift, some demonstration of care and sympathy—these are the needs of our world; these are the wares of genuine religion.

The open secret of many tall-statured souls consists in taking time to perform the unheralded services for the downtrodden, to champion unpopular causes, and to right some flagrant, unpublicized wrong. To sit where they sit, to walk in another man's shoes, to enter into his grief and trials, to shoulder another's burdens, to bear another's cross, to endure another's thorn—ah, these are the actions which faith demands in its insistence on following the lowly Galilean. He took on Himself the miseries of the whole human race. This, our day of opportunity, needs the empathy of Ezekiel, the steadfastness of Paul, the objectiveness of a Samaritan, and the vision of the prophet John. But most of all, we need the selfless love of the Son of God if we are to transfuse the sickly millions who are ready to give up and call life a shoddy spectacle.

Life Is Worth Living as Long as One Untrodden Path Remains

There is a holy romance about the unknown, the ever-beckoning magnet toward new horizons. So long as one fresh, untrodden path is left for human feet, then no one need give up.

A sterile falsehood is everywhere in evidence among modern men: the belief that the best poetry has been written, the finest music already composed, and that both renaissance and reformation belong to the archives of history. Not so! The few lines of poetic value suggest that they are a nucleus of a reservoir of verse awaiting human conception and expression. Melodic tones and the whole repertoire of expressions are but a few notes compared to what could and should be done for the ear of man and God. The threshold of a greater reformation is always imminent when the right *reformer* is in pursuit of it. A renaissance of culture among the sordid vulgarity of this day and generation is a prime necessity. Who says life isn't worth living so long as we have nothing more than a yeoman's conception of the human intellect, the untrammelled canals of the mind, and the projection of spirit into unknown worlds?

Life Is Worth Living When Divine Purpose Is Discovered

Human nature receives its fullest abundance when it drinks from the well of divine purpose for an individual's life. Then life becomes a sacred score, played to God's own liking and for His distinctive glory. Herein one can hold on when gloom, ill fortune, evil and tyranny possess the land; herein is the strongest endorsement for continuity.

When a person comes under the compulsion of divine purpose, he gets up and gets out from under the juniper tree of pity; he makes tracks even in the desert sands as he remembers there are other oases on the road to accomplishment.

The dust of defeatism trails far behind as his pace is accelerated, moving with direction and dispatch. Knowing that he never walks alone, then loneliness is seldom his lot. His is the assurance of Whittier's "Eternal Goodness":

> I know not what the future hath
> Of marvel or surprise,
> Assured alone that life and death
> His mercy underlies.[2]

The Human-Divine Role in Escaping Darkness

If a person standing at life's danger point is able to summon all the resources within himself, declaring total effort to pull out of it,

[2] John Greenleaf Whittier, "The Eternal Goodness."

even this is not sufficient. Humanism has left its corrosive half-truths in the fabric of modern thinking, a fact which explains the ease of shunting God to one side in the problem situations. Read the list of proposed cures for mental sickness, or for moral collapse and its attendant vices—lists proposed by experts in the field—and see how many overlook the major source of man's hope and help: God. This is not to say that man is to lean on his Maker while expending no effort to help himself. It is, however, an admission that self-help falls miserably short of achieving the desired results.

What can distracted, guilt-ridden man count on so far as God is concerned? To what extent will He lead us out of the dark? The right answers to these questions will determine the quality and quantity of our health.

THREE BASIC FACTS CONCERNING GOD'S ACTIVITY IN MAN'S PROBLEMS

I. God Never Closes a Door Without Raising a Window

An American soldier, fatally wounded one minute before the Cease-Fire in Korea, said before he died, "Isn't that just like God!" To think of God in terms of such cruelty is to make Him a tyrant who crushes man's fondest dreams. Regardless of the stress under which a person reasons, it is neither truthful nor fair to judge God from a low perspective. God is no sadist who delights in our dark nights and cloudy days. A long time ago Isaiah asked, "To whom then shall we liken our God?" What is He really like?

Jesus revealed God as a loving Father actively involved in His world through the Holy Spirit. One of the major religions has ninety-nine names for God, but "Father" is not one of them. From one's father can be expected the loving provisions which life requires. But at the point of providing for our needs—physical, emotional, spiritual—God has a difficult time. Not that He is limited by inability, but because we limit Him by our doubts and wavering attitudes. For Him to get His way with most of us involves a long process of closing doors and raising windows.

93

The doors that are closed seem to be an insult, especially when we have chosen specific ones through which we are determined to go. Now and again we come to that place in life when, after we have prayed for something specific to happen—a job to open, a disease to be healed, a set of circumstances to be changed—things do not work out the way we have asked. God is saying in effect, "I closed the door through which you tried to go so that I could guide you down life's hallway to the door through which I want you to go." Too often, the situation resembles that of a young couple who employed an architect and contractor to build their new home. However, from the first day, the eager couple proceeded to change the plans, demanding that a wall be moved, a door and window unit changed, and other costly alterations be made. Hampered and heckled, the contractor finished the job with a sigh of relief. When God says that certain gables do not fit life's architecture, and particular choices are no complement to a unified way of living, He is not being dictatorial—He is being life's best architect.

Most killing tensions stem from man's wanting to be his own architect and contractor, to build his life by and for himself. The beauty of a Christlike life consists in a childlike willingness to follow divine guidance, acknowledging God as the only One who sees our tomorrow. Some will still say, "I have surrendered my life but just look: it seems as though I am locked in a dark room with no way to turn. Where is all the evidence that everything would work out for good?" What evidence is needed? It takes time—God hasn't promised to remove all problems just because we number ourselves in His company. He has promised to do something better: to accept the problems in accordance with His purpose and plan.

God closed dungeon doors on John Bunyan but simultaneously opened a window through which the lines of *Pilgrim's Progress* streamed. He closed doors on Martin Niemöller, yet windows were opened to let through a shaft of divine light. A providentially slammed door for an Alsatian youth, caused a window to be opened in Lambaréné, illuminating that part of dark Africa with an unextinguishable light.

This accommodating goodness of God showed its real profile when a Norwegian fisherman with his two sons went on their daily fishing run. As usual, the mother went down to the wharf to see her family off and wish them safety and a good catch. By mid-afternoon the waves were rolling higher than usual. A sharp, brisk wind whipped little spits of salty spray into the faces of the rugged man and his teen-age boys. The wind increased, the waves grew like humped, marine giants of a prehistoric day. The storm caused the little boat to toss and pitch as the three rowed desperately to get back to shore. The fierce storm put out the light in the lighthouse on shore, leaving the fishermen dependent upon dark, groping guesswork.

Meanwhile, in the kitchen of their rustic cottage a fire broke out. Before the wife and mother could put out the fire, it destroyed their every earthly possession except the clothes on their backs. Finally, the father and sons were able to row the boat safely to shore. Waiting on the beach to tell them the tragic news of the fire was the wife and mother. "Karl," she tearfully said, "fire has destroyed our house and all our possessions. We have nothing now." But Karl seemed strangely unmoved by the disconcerting news. "Didn't you hear me, Karl? Our house is gone." "Yes, I heard you," he replied, "but a few hours ago we were lost at sea, riding high waves and death seemed mighty close. Our only guide to the shoreline, the light in the house on the cliff, went out. For an hour I thought death would be our lot. Then something happened: a dim, yellow glow appeared in the distance. Then it grew bigger and bigger. We turned our boat and rowed with all our might to get in the path of that light. When we did, we followed it safely to the shore. You see, Ingrid," he explained, "that little yellow glow was the first sight of our house burning. At the peak of the blaze, we could see that shoreline as bright as day. The same heat that destroyed our house, created a light which saved our lives."

Just so with many of the doors that shut in our face for no apparent reason. At such times if we would exercise enough faith to wait and see, most times God would point His index finger down life's hallway to a double door, standing wide open, through which He wants us to go.

95

> Keep a brave spirit, and never despair;
> Hope brings you messages through the air;
> God is victorious—God everywhere.[3]

II. Though God Will Bend He Will Never Break Us

It is a compliment that all of man's relations with God are not pleasant. Some involve rigors of chastening and discipline which leave the faithless prostrate and cynical. If one will walk with God far enough, he will find that God will bend him but will never break him. This is a divine promise: "A bruised reed he will not break, a smoking flax he will not quench." Life's reeds can be bent to the ground by ill-blowing winds. Still, the guarantee from above is that the reeds will not be broken in the process. Herein is a beautiful facet of divine nature. Pagan societies have reasoned that the aged, infirm, impotent, maimed and blind members of the human race were useless to society and should be denied a right to live. In Hitler's plan for the world such pathetic sufferers were to have been liquidated. But in the economy of God's Kingdom there is provision for all, room for everyone. No, just because age and adversity approach, there is no basis for concluding that God ultimately will break you.

The community of elderly people increases all the time. The "miracle" drugs, finer diets, and healthier working conditions are adding years to the span of life. But if individuals do not bring to life a worthwhile attitude and purpose, of what value are additional years? Prolonged uselessness is more of a curse than a blessing.

Let the real truth be told: God cares for that increasing number who feel left out, even if society does not care. And while He permits one to be bent by many trying circumstances, He will not permit the bending to be excessive—never to the point of breaking.

This treasured truth also applies to personal temptation. No-one shall be tempted beyond his ability to withstand. This is God's promise too. What a blow such a truth is to the sorry fight many put up in resisting temptation. Someone usually says, "This habit is

[3] Attributed to an anonymous minister of Scotland in the eighteenth century.

beyond me; I cannot control it. Seems as though God has singled me out with such a weakness; why am I so weak?" Then follows a litany of self-pity which dramatizes temptation while rushing to embrace it.

God doesn't tempt anyone to sin. The prayer that Jesus taught His disciples to pray, "Lead us not into temptation," needs to be interpreted so that everyone is clearly convinced that God never takes the initiative in leading a single soul to temptation. He permits us to be led but stands in Spartan awareness when we have had enough.

God's bending is for a purpose. Until metal is subjected to heat it has no resiliency. A kite does not rise with the wind, but against it. A plane is kept aloft in the air by downdrafts and up-pulls. Man's soul is polished by abrasive sands which irritate, aggravate, but also create a brilliant lustre. While the ladder of life is full of splinters, few ever get pricked by them except those who slide down. Some folks fail to see the beautiful roses because they look at the thorns on them; others thank God that thorns have roses.

At a dark time of the War Between the States, one of the governors wrote a letter of gloom and despair to Lincoln. The brief reply he received read "Dick, stand still and see the salvation of the Lord."

III. Man's Extremity Can Be God's Best Opportunity

What a commentary—that man must come to his lowest estate before reaching out his faltering hand to God! There is an ignoble note in emergency religion. Holy Writ records only one instance of deathbed repentance, and this for two reasons: that man may not despair—it is possible; but that man may not presume—it is highly improbable. The easiest way is to cry, "O God," when one can do no other. Desperation is a poor altar, and fear is an ignoble motive for surrender.

Still, there is something to be said about man's extremities: Dire circumstances provide God with proper entry and man with the right mood of dependance for redemption. When one is down and out, at least God doesn't have to contend with pride in order to help.

97

"Blessed are the poor in spirit." Why? Because they don't have any-thing and they *know* they don't. These are more apt to admit spiritual poverty than those who can write a check for anything they desire, while admitting no need for divine help.

Why must there be an eleventh-hour coming to God? When energies are gone, fortunes wasted on indulgent living, minds left uncultured in the graces of magnanimous living, if we then offer God the leftovers, there is very little to bring God in old age except infirmities, groans and strains. This is the reason most of my efforts are channeled in the direction of young people. They have their lives before them and when they live for God and Christ, long years of devotion accrue to the world's account.

Life has no depths beyond the reach of God, no heights that out-stretch Him, no secret places that elude His searching eyes. Re-membering this fact should enable many to forego the extreme crisis which places men out of the immediate reach of love's prox-imity. Only after the thief had been crucified did he cry out to Christ for help. Only after the prodigal son had spent his days in riotous living did he feel the nature of the hogs' company and turn toward his father's house.

In the shade of a juniper tree Elijah saw the depth of despair. The woman at a Palestinian well never quite realized what depths illicit living could bring until Christ's presence enabled her to see in His honest light. Jonah, in the depths of the sea, found God was present in emergencies. Man's extremities sometimes are God's best opportunities.

When I was a young boy, I went swimming one day with another boy about my age. The old "wash" hole in the creek was swift and swirling after a heavy July rain. Hardly had we entered the water before I heard my friend calling for help. He had drifted into a whirlpool that spun him around like a top. Down he went. My efforts to help him were clumsy and he almost drowned both of us. An uncle, seeing our plight, jumped in the swirling water and wrestled with the boy as both went under time and again. Then it happened: with a heavy blow of his fist in the boy's face, his uncle knocked him out. The unconscious lad was pulled to safety and revived on the bank. Not until the boy's frantic, awkward desperation was overridden was he saved. The same is true for some men and women in their relation to God. Not until some dire extremity comes their way will they permit God to save them.

Today, America is riding a white horse of prosperity and plenty. We are of all people most blessed. On deposit in our banks is more money than any citizens have ever owned before. Constituting only 6 per cent of the world's population, we consume over half the world's goods and services. Now: why should we have to be brought to catastrophe, with all its excruciating involvements, before we turn to God? Why not acknowledge Him at high noon instead of midnight? This would mark us as nobler people.

SUMMARY

To a great extent we determine the density of the dark as well as its duration. Rather than cursing the darkness which has settled over the world, there is a supply of candles which we could light. A little light will dispel a lot of darkness. You might be surprised what God would add to that single flicker with His own limitless resources of illumination, if you would go ahead and light the candle of your influence.

At the lowest moment of his despair, William Cowper rode over London looking for the river into which he had planned to plunge. Fog was so thick that night that he rode in the horse-drawn cab for an hour or more. Life had run into the short rows of meaninglessness, futility, and hopelessness. To end it all seemed the better part of valor and wisdom. But where was the river? Rebuking the cabbie for taking so long to find the river bank, Cowper thrust open the door of his cab. Upon doing so, he discovered that instead of being near the river, he was right back at his own doorstep! That did it. Smitten by such singular coincidence, he rushed to his room, took a quill and paper and penned the lines that have cheered millions who have come to the brink of disaster.

> God moves in a mysterious way
> His wonders to perform;

He plants His footsteps in the sea,
And rides upon the storm.

Deep in unfathomable mines
Of never-failing skill
He treasures up His bright designs,
And works His sovereign will.

Ye fearful saints, fresh courage take;
The clouds ye so much dread
Are big with mercy, and shall break
In blessings on your head.

Judge not the Lord by feeble sense,
But trust Him for His grace;
Behind a frowning providence
He hides a smiling face.

His purposes will ripen fast,
Unfolding every hour;
The bud may have a bitter taste
But sweet will be the flower.

Blind unbelief is sure to err,
And scan His work in vain;
God is His own interpreter
And He will make it plain.[4]

[4] William Cowper, "Light Shining Out of Darkness."

If I
Should
Die 5
Before
I Live

Genuine living is not in doing what you like, but in liking what you do.

"Whoever loses his life for my sake, he will save it."—Jesus Christ

As LITTLE CHILDREN we were taught a simple prayer, one line of which said, "If I should die before I wake. . . ." I was grown before realizing the real wisdom of that single line. If I should die before I wake—up to live! This is not only an "if" clause concerning death; it is the biggest subjunctive of life. If I should die before I have really come alive to the things that matter in time and eternity. . . . Who am I? From whence did I come? Why am I living? These are the real questions that mark the difference between sensitive awareness and dull apathy. It is easy to mark off days and years in meaningless routine and come to the end with no sense of conviction that life has been a progressive revelation of struggle and triumph and purposeful planning. Instead, the final conclusion for many is that living out one's days really isn't worth the effort involved.

The wondrous truth about the way of life that Jesus taught and exemplified is that being a Christian not only prepares one to die, but equips one to live here and now, as well as hereafter. It is both insurance for death and assurance for life—eternal. " 'Tis heaven below my Redeemer to know." If one doesn't learn the triumphant art of living superlatively on earth, what role could heaven possibly play in such a life hereafter? To infer that one who plods through life has an inherent right to immortality is to vulgarize heaven while ignoring the gospel truth. No, eternal life is not the natural endowment of mankind. Rather, it is a free gift of

101

God to those who are twice-born, and who, by virtue of membership in the heavenly family, bring their lives into line with the perfect guide—Jesus Christ.

Either seeing another life that has come alive in God, or surveying the sorry wreckage of his own, often will prod a person to confess, "I have made a failure of life. If I had my life to live over . . . ." Then follows the usual, well-intentioned but untruthful declaration that all sorts of circumstances would be different. Perhaps it is being too honest to tell such folk that if they had their time to live over, in all probability they would live it again much as they did the first time. A more jolting truth is the unarguable fact that no one has his life to live over. It is a one-way street for all: poets, cynics, philosophers, saints and sinners!

At a time in history when two European nations were gripped in revolutionary throes of nationalism, many people were victimized by political forces which desperately held on to the reigns of government. Heads toppled in the civil embattlements. During that heated bid for freedom, one man wrote his former colleague in Britain: "You asked in a letter how things were going with us. I am happy to report that things are going well. The old system is breaking up. New hope is on the horizon that men shall be free. In the process many are losing their heads, but the price isn't too high for freedom. Many are losing their heads—come and lend us yours."

Just such a time is the day in which we live. Old systems are crumbling, old alliances and allegiances are being filed in dusty archives of days and events gone by. What a time to be alive! And though some may lose their heads in the process, let the severance result from intelligent principles for which they stood, rather than foolhardiness and vain ambition.

This chapter attempts to contrast dull, purposeless existence on one hand with superlative, abundant, radiant living on the other. If life is half as interesting as Jesus taught it to be, then we should seize life as a torch, holding it high so that the stumbling, human race can see where it is going. Blind groping for the light intensifies the darkness. The world's greatest surplus is darkness; the light bearers must not add to that surplus.

WHEN DEATH PRECEDES LIFE—A PORTRAIT OF LIFE WITHOUT LUSTRE

A teen-age girl was lovingly tended for thirteen months following a tragic accident. Fed intravenously, she lay in a comatose state with no indication that she was living, except for breathing. With no conscious awareness, no response to natural stimuli, no exercise, a bare minimum of bodily functions, she just lay there much like a corpse. It is possible for man to exist in a world of beauty, color, consuming interests and activities, without any response or reaction of a constructive nature; endless opportunities may be regarded with a jaundiced eye of suspicion, while the chance to get involved is permitted to slip by without regard. Tides of challenge ebb and rise for this type of human exister, but he sees both ebb and flood tide as one and the same.

BOREDOM: THE INEVITABLE ALLY

There are few exceptions to the rule that one who marks off his days in uselessness becomes both bored and a bore. Seeing no real meaning in life, he scowls and accuses. Inbred thoughts never widen the circumference of his outlook. Naturally, the same old prejudices, the slick-worn jokes and figures of speech, the same cased-in choices and inclinations can be expected. Inevitably, his circle of friends gradually narrows, until old age finds him on an island of loneliness, chronic despair and sourness. The church still has some responsibility to this kind, though the value of their lives to the Kingdom is negligible because most of them remain in an uncommitted, selfish detachment, ineffectual witnesses for God's truth and Christ's way of life!

The most familiar profile in America is a typically successful businessman or woman whose life is lived without eternal overtones. Simple souls preferring freedom from elaboration with no controversial involvement, they follow the lines of least resistance. No heroic adventure lures them from their stodgy lives. Playing it

103

safely, they refuse to gamble with the dynamic truth that nothing is impossible to a believer. To such people, every ship seems romantic except the one on which they sail. Religion is often little more than confirmation of caution.

As a little band of hunters listened to instructions from their guide, he stated, "You will encounter many hazards on this safari: insects, reptiles, swollen rivers, vicious animals, but nothing will be more hazardous than the mires of quicksand. Be on your guard for these placid spots. They are yawning chasms of death." The journey through life has its quicksand, its snares for unwary, unheeding feet. Since many "guides" have set themselves to the infamous job of camouflaging some of the sand mires, alertness is even more in order. The fact that deception in subtle, well-financed form is on the bound today makes it even more urgent that no man go through life with a heedless attitude.

The sin of nothingness is a crime all its own. To believe that life is a sheer accident, a set of contradictory circumstances without design, purpose, or plan does not mark a person as well-informed. It may mean that he is stupid. What right has a person to go through God's world as a snobbish critic of all that he sees without expending some effort to improve instead of criticizing? Of all the freedoms that accrue to his account, I contend, this is not one of them. God sent His Son into the world to live and die for it. For a man to regard that with a casual "what-does-it-matter" attitude is the vilest type of indifference—a life of nothingness.

Today millions of people have as their sole purpose to get by, to seek out a few creature comforts, to extract what they can without putting much, if anything, back into the world. Actually, this is the nature and activity of a parasite. Having no roots of its own, a parasitic plant must draw from another plant, tree or organism, its life's sustenance. Into this family fit leeches, mistletoe and people who intentionally live on "welfare."

How can a person live in this kind of world, with all its wondrous opportunities for enlightenment, its uncharted horizons, its locked-up freedoms, its aggravatingly alluring designs, its magnetic poles of consuming thought, its rarefied virtues, highly esteemed but rarely exemplified, its beckoning vistas, its alluring challenges—how can one live in this kind of world and remain stolidly neutral? The fact that some can is a compounded mystery. When applied to professing Christians, this mystery is even more acute. In the self-effacing rigors of Christian discipleship, not one adherent is to remain a passive spectator. By virtue of his association and identification, he is automatically a participator—or at least, he is supposed to be. No one who goes under the ensign of Christ's name has liberty to go through long periods of neutrality in service, where interest wanes and zeal drags. The little typed reminder on train tickets, "No Good If Detached," applies also to those who number themselves among the redeemed—no good if detached from the body of Christian believers. God has no Christians Anonymous.

What a reassuring, inspiring sight to see a life committed to that which is the highest in holiness! One who is willing to spend and be spent in the greatest cause on earth, especially a young person, clean faced, high browed, pure hearted, whose shoulder is tight against life's wheel, is a sight that transfixes and transforms.

"Why doesn't he clear his throat and speak out clearly?" an irked visitor asked another sitting on the church pew beside him. Before an answer could be given, the displeasure of the questioner became more apparent as the preacher continued. This man of God, having served as pastor of that little church for two decades, had suffered a severe throat condition which had necessitated a number of operations. The last one left his vocal cords weak and easily exhausted. Sometimes it was almost impossible for people to hear him. "Why don't you get a new minister?" was the second question thrown at the unanswering worshiper. Finally, the man answered, "This man's life is his best sermon, and we just love to see him go in his pulpit." What a compliment; what an encouragement for keeping on when every argument is on the side of giving up!

FILLED CHURCHES—EMPTY PEOPLE?

Daily soul-searching is in order among church leaders to reconcile an apparent contradiction: Filled churches, but churches filled with comparatively empty people. Thronged gatherings, but relatively few crosses; multitudes at the doors, dwindling minorities at denials; religion in abundance, Christianity in scarcity; brotherhood daily proclaimed and hourly denied—is this overstating the case? We must not forget that history's impersonal finger points to many painters but not to many artists. Millions are studying music but how many are great musicians? Mere possesssion of tools and a union card does not make a man a carpenter. And in like reasoning, neither does singing doxologies, contributing to cash drives, nor pale smiles of assent to theolological dogma make one a Christian. When Jesus said, "Few there be that find it," referring to the strait gate and narrow path to eternal life, He meant exactly what He said. The quality kind of life found in Him does not come by easy rote. It is the result of long, arduous effort based on unmerited grace. Never has the rank and file of humanity been interested enough to survey the dimensions of the gate, let alone make the ego humble enough to fit the gate's dimensions.

But many quickly object to this reasoning by pointing to the limelight of favorable acceptance in which organized religion basks. Why, it is the thing to do to belong to the church. Everybody is doing it, and isn't that reason enough to justify the conclusion that, despite the rigorous talk of early ascetics about crosses, denials and such things, the modern route of low presssure and cushions is to be preferred? Hardly! Among other errors, such reasoning gives rise to an inflated sense of self-importance contending that the church must have certain people belong to it. This is as erroneous as saying that the air needs people to breathe it. The very opposite is true!

"IT MIGHT HAVE BEEN"

> For of all sad words of tongue or pen,
> The saddest are these: "It might have
> been!"[1]

It is sad indeed to view a life that possessed the raw material of accomplishment but never refined it, never made anything of it— a might-have-been.

[1] John Greenleaf Whittier, "Maud Muller." Stanza 53.

This post-mortem wisdom showed up in epitaph form on a tombstone in Scotland. Composed in jest, it comes frighteningly close to realism:

"Born a human being—died a wholesale grocer."

Are the two antithetic—a human being and a grocer? Many times, tragically, they are. When life is bent to the altars of accounting sheets, working all day on Sunday, using up the last ounce of energy in order to fuel the fires of mammon, then something happens inside a man's soul. This is present-day obsession. Modern education must come in for its share of blame for teaching techniques without doing much for the technician, for giving rise to a generation of nuclear giants who, in many cases, are moral infants. Phi Beta Kappa scientists but spiritual duds; those who know all the hypotheses but never come to a knowledge of the Truth. Financial millionaires but spiritual paupers! Born a human being; died a successful businessman. So what? God put us here to serve Him, not to line our pockets in selfish acquisition while living out our days as egomaniacs.

Luigi Corneglio died after seventy years of poverty. Most of those years were spent begging. The outstretched hand was his trademark. In an old, cheap tenement they found his body after it had lain dead three days among dirty rags and papers yellowed with age. From all appearances, here was an old man who had nothing and came to a monotonously familiar pauper's death. Not so. For in the attic of the dirty tenement, forty-seven violins were found, one of which was an expensive Stradivarius. Think of it: A priceless violin lying still and silent in a miser's attic. That instrument wasn't made to collect dust or to be taken out of circulation by hoarding hands. It was made to be played, to speak in mellow notes of beauty. For that matter, neither was Corneglio made to join the dirty rags and trash of life. Music was in him too, but he never got it out of him. Collecting musical instruments became twice a sin to him. He neither became a musician himself, nor did he make the violins available to those who were musicians. Cobwebs and dusty rafters are inappropriate props for a Stradivarius! Colorless, staid existence is poor fare for a man made in the image of God, who is capable of something better.

THE SIN OF BEING ORDINARY

A previous generation used some common phraseology that has fallen into disuse today. When asked about their general state of being, many older people had a habit of saying, "I am sorta po'ly today." "Po'ly." By that word they meant that things were not going so well, that their state of health, mind or circumstance was in the "so-so" bracket; neither tragically bad nor particularly good. This can be the state of spiritual circumstances in one's life, and that state can become his real nature. Being "so-so" Christians, living a "po'ly" life, means contentment with the sin of being ordinary. The same thing is involved when we refer to "average" people: average Americans, average church members, average students. By this term we mean: nothing outstanding, run-of-the-mill, just ordinary.

There is an ironic commentary on Methuselah in the Bible. He wins the laurels of longevity, yet, despite his nearly one thousand years of existence, all the record says about him is, "And Methuselah lived 969 years and died." What a record! A thousand years was a mighty long time to live. But all the author of Genesis had to say about him was a comment on his length of days.

Contrast his life with that of Christ's. One man lived less than forty years but look at His accomplishments. Few biographers refer to His span of years, for the very good reason that the least valuable index of real living is longevity. It is possible for some to pack more intense, qualitative living in one year than others do in a lifetime. One hour of superlative inspiration is worth more to God's Kingdom and man's soul than decades of dull monotonous marking off of days. Living a little less than four decades, here was a solitary figure who never knew the joy of bouncing His own son on His lap. He never owned a piece of real estate, knew nothing about the modern comforts of air-conditioning, automation, fast transportation, never sat in an airplane nor rode an elevator. He probably didn't travel outside His native country. He was not conversant with foreign lands, for His was not the luxury of extended traveling. Nor could He boast of many formal degrees since His schooling was

108

limited to the synagogue instruction in a small village. Being of a humble, poor family, He knew nothing of the social register and its often vaunted prerogatives which open doors of opportunities unknown to the less fortunate. He didn't have the inside track with the ruling powers of His day, He didn't know the big shots whose influence was deemed imperative to most other men with things to be done. This man Jesus laid no claim to material possessions even as means to a noble end. Believing that God would provide life's essentials, He seemed to ignore the haunting, hounding mania for more, an obsession apparent among most others in His day. He had no military service to His credit.

Yet, in the long annals of historical biographies, search wherever you will, no man will remotely approximate in achievement—all fields of human endeavor included—this single, solitary Man of Galilee. From ordinary circumstances He produced extraordinary results; from average conditions came unprecedented accomplishments. He took common people and led them to uncommon heights. Fishermen, tax collectors, tenders of sheep and goats, ragged children, leprous and nameless outcasts, despised harlots, feared and fearful mentally sick—these constituted the motley lot among whom Jesus worked, loved and died.

Had He possessed the strategic resources of noble birth, the leverage of material wealth, the inside track of political and social preferment; had He had the entrée of academic endorsement so that the well-informed would have rallied to His call; had these been His tools, what He was able to do would still defy imagination. But lacking these "advantages" and accomplishing what He did forces only one conclusion: God was in Christ reconciling the world unto Himself.

With this example before us, man has no right to be content with little gains, ordinary achievements, and so-so actions. Sinning? Indeed, because any goal short of God's ordained goal for an individual's life, and the forces which make one fall short of that goal, is sinning.

An early Greek general, looking over a conglomerate array of men who had been hastily conscripted for military service, remarked to his lieutenant, "Would that I had as many soldiers as I have men." No doubt God has wished the same thing when surveying the multitudes of ordinary plodders who call themselves Christians: "Would that I had as many Christians as I have church members."

Imagine the confused amazement when the relatives of a Finnish infidel met to hear his will read. The next of kin sat silent as death, since they couldn't even guess what the wishes of the infidel farmer would be. In one simple sentence he left his earthly possessions, consisting solely of a big farm, to one recipient: the devil! After deliberation, and no contesting of the will, the court decided that the best way to carry out the infidel farmer's wishes was to leave the farm alone. Let none till the soil or control erosion, no hands kill the weeds, no one harvest. Just let it lie idle. In a few years the acres were grown over. Briars, weeds, creeping vines clutched at every fruit tree, while gullies washed the topsoil into the streams. The buildings faded, and decayed. Truly, it went to the devil by default, neglect and waste.

Eroding minds, unpainted attitudes, thorny prejudices, serpentine tempers and ordinary, run-of-the-mill dispositions send many a person to a similar fate. This ought not to be!

THE MENACE OF MEDIOCRITY

The sin of ordinariness leads to a set of circumstances in which human personality resigns itself to the menace of mediocrity in a process by which life is reduced to its lowest common denominator. Being part and parcel of a "getting by" attitude, mediocrity and its ugly children account for so much of our frustrative tensions. With enough self-respect left to activate a pinch of guilt when one does settle for less than his best, such a person is torn in two directions: on one hand is a summons for qualitative effort; on the other hand lies the easy rationalization, "Since one can't do it all in a lifetime anyway, why try so hard to do all that is possible?" Usually, this is all that is needed to stifle extra effort.

Perhaps nothing mirrors the mediocrity of modern man so clearly as our attitude toward work. It no longer is respectable to sweat! A punch-the-clock regard is standard procedure for multi-millions. Getting by with the bare minimum; living, or rather, existing, between coffee or tea breaks; stopping the machine thirty minutes before quitting time—these attitudes and actions never appear to the ones involved as dishonesty or laziness. Who put out the yarn that work will kill you? None is known to have worked himself or herself to death—all contentions to the contrary. But the energy expended by those mediocre souls in the process of avoiding work would harness many horses and power big generators.

The scope and magnitude of mediocrity is seen in many facets of our society. Education is at fault, with its bare minimum requirements, its surrender to "progressive" projects at the expense of solid learning, its decrying of firm discipline while witnessing a generation of wild, undisciplined youth believing that the world owes them a living and that they will have what they want regardless of methods or consequences—education that refuses to strait-jacket the human mind in that rigorous, painful though necessary routine of concentrative effort.

Our assembly-line produced gadgets, our cheap imitations of the old masters, our dime-store plastic and paper facsimiles, these speak of folks with a five-and-ten-cent outlook on life, who see no sense in searching through the old, dusty attics for some real work of art when one "just as good" can be bought at the five-and-ten.

The church must come in for a scathing indictment at this point: a menacing mediocrity that has no place in church life shows its ugly face in many activities. Programs poorly planned, music ineffectually rendered, sermons often substituting noise for content, goals too low for tall-standing souls, and visions devoid of wonder and romance—these are in evidence on every hand. It is expecting too much from the populace to think they will respond to second-rate, warmed-over rations served in an atmosphere of ecclesiastical stodginess. Neither duty nor demanded loyalties can suffer such unpalatable diet for long.

It is too easy to reason that a commonplace, mediocre church program is the result of our having too much to do, or because

111

we can't afford certain tools or adequate personnel for the job. Many well-endowed people fall short of real living so far as the church is concerned, not because of inability, but because of unwillingness to contribute the right amount of time and energy. Just because one is a resounding success, say, in finance, doesn't qualify him to be a Bible teacher. Acceptance for leadership in community affairs is no qualification for leadership on the official board of a church. In each case one must cultivate the art of willing commitment of life's endowments to God's use. Others, whose endowments are few and fragmentary, fail to put what they have at God's disposal because they feel slighted. Believing that God short-changed them when He passed around the talents, they go through life with a self-penalizing disposition. The real lesson to be learned in this case is that God doesn't dole out gifts indiscriminately, nor does He give them all at once. If a person feels himself to be endowed in a niggardly fashion, then the best recourse is to invest what he does have, and the promise is that he will gain. Seeing a willingness to use present possessions, God sends other gifts. In tandem these follow just as long as a man wants to play the game with God. So, today's one-talent man can be tomorrow's two-talent person. Next year the same person will be even farther along. A decade from now that original talent, like money put in good stock, can double, or quadruple. Proof? Just look around you at the people who have taken God at His word and made something of themselves.

Right here, however, I must raise a word of warning. Life has to follow God's design for investment if it is to pay off compound interest. It would be gross dishonesty to imply that a dullard can start coming to church, give his money, think positively, and become a genius! But he can become his maximum self when his efforts are under divine tutelage.

This lesson was set in sharp focus when I started to study typing. Before enrolling in a business school, I knew a hunt-and-peck system which had made possible a fair degree of speed. The worst difficulty I encountered in learning to type the right way was unlearning my hunt-and-peck system. Fingers that were accustomed to certain keys were assigned new letters. Muscles conditioned to reach in one direction had to be reconditioned. Finally, I acquired

112

a speed of a hundred words a minute, but only after learning the correct method. Just so with life in God. Man must give up his hunt-and-peck technique before he can master any speed with God's method and will.

"HE DIED ON THIRD BASE"

It was nearing the last inning of the ball game and a tense crowd kept calling for a home run. A player on third base was the best bet for a score. But he refused to take chances; he stuck closely to the mound that marked the base. And the game ended, scoreless. In the game of life many people come up to bat; gripping it with full might, they swing hard and the ball rises to left field. The hit good for a three-base run, the player feels a surge of elation as the crowds shout approval. Then something happens: time passes and enthusiasms wane. Relying on the next batter to bring him home, he fails to run the risks involved in sliding home by arduous effort and shrewd calculation. Preferring the safety of the ground covered, he sticks to his base. The game ends and no score is made. The short-lived glory of running three-fourths of the way means nothing if one doesn't come all the way. The writer of the Epistle to the Galatians asked such an one who died on third base, "You were running well, what has hindered you?"

AND NOW: TO LIVE WHILE EXISTING— PRESCRIPTIONS FOR PURPOSEFULNESS

Now we face the privilege of a happy affirmation: life is worth living and part of the process involves the romantic mystery of answering the question, When does a person really live? How can I know that I am realizing at least part of my potential for God? Is length of days any indication? Hardly. Longevity is no ultimate measure of worth. Living long may be little more than prolongation of misery or uselessness. The length of a rope does not determine its tensile strength nor do length of days necessarily deposit anything to the account of resourceful living.

Is happiness a criterion of successful living? Not when pleasure is equated with happiness. In such a case the combination may equal nothing more than sensuality. Epicureans would have been the superlative exemplars had this been a worthy yardstick of living. Happiness always is a by-product of a nobler pursuit than pleasure.

What is the real measure of quality living? Growth! One lives only when he grows. Stop growing and life ceases. The minute the body reaches maturity, a cycle commences in which it starts dying. Though slow and imperceptible, it is dying nonetheless. Old age creeps stealthily onward. In like manner, when growth is arrested in mind and spirit, the process of functional rigor mortis is under way. Stagnation and sterility invite the bitter scythe of death.

The teen-age girl who was in a comatose state for over a year, referred to earlier in this chapter, came back to normalcy. After thirteen months of immobility, there was a slight flicker of bodily movement. Her eyes opened; she whispered a sound. In a few weeks she was walking, smiling, singing. When human life encounters Jesus Christ in the experience of salvation, it is as though that one had been dead and has come back to life. In fact, it is a rebirth, a being born into a new world and a new family relationship. Life wakes up—it comes alive to eternal realities.

Let Jesus describe it: "I came that they might have life, and that they might have it more abundantly." Abundantly—the richest adverb in the Bible! It is rich in overflowing, intelligent compensation for effort, in day-by-day challenges and in year-by-year rebukes and reassurances. Life in Jesus Christ almost resents passing of time, while holding time in relative insignificance since it knows that real citizenship is not in time but in eternity.

Song in the Soul

Life is set to music when redemption is set in action. Where discord and noise were amplified in the unrepentant state of existence, now harmonies and melodic chords of words and deeds abound. Dissonance and off-beat cymbals are replaced by more welcomed tones of harps and violins.

Song in the soul! That is what vital, relevant religion means. Thrown in a Philippian jail, Paul and Silas had every right to feel sorry for themselves. Their crime? The simple preaching of eternal truth. But that truth was more than some first-century officials could bear, so these two disciples were whipped and locked in a dirty jail. But what a strange reaction they showed! At midnight they woke the other prisoners by singing. Singing at midnight! Were they drunk? Yes, an inebriation distinctively its own: drunk on the power and presence of Almighty God. Their souls had been set to music and it had to come out. What a blessed alternative to the gloom and despondency which demands that life give up at such times. There they were: penniless, with their backs bleeding and their future one dark uncertainty, but their state of mind triumphant.

There was an humble man who had two consuming loves: music and God. He served both with no split-level loyalties. Working hard all his life, he came to the end of his days unappreciated even by his close neighbors. He thought of himself as an arduous worker, doing his work regardless of popularity or financial strictures. Next-door neighbors regarded him as about as important as the local merchant or cobbler. His snobbish musician sons looked down their noses on their father as "that old peruke." But that "old peruke," Johann Sebastian Bach, would probably be voted by most musicians today as the greatest composer of them all.

It took expert, dedicated musicians forty-six years to gather all his music, and they had filled sixty huge, printed volumes when they had completed the task. A present-day scribe would have to work seventy years just to write down all the scores the way Bach did—and he composed them, too! Did he really live? Well, let's see. When but a lad of nine, already there was a consuming hunger to know and compose. He lived with a tyrannical, older brother and wife. Denied the privilege of using his brother's musical library, young Bach crept in after the others were asleep and copied music by moonlight. Eventually, he copied every note of instrumental music by hand. When his brother found the laboriously copied scores, he burned them! This did not deter Johann at all. Using every opportunity that resourceful sweat provided, the genius within him came out under adverse circumstances. Bach died in

1750 with little acclaim and was buried in an unmarked grave in a Leipzig churchyard.

One of his sons started selling his father's musical works, some of them for as little as ten cents a score. What propelled the man to continue in the face of such staggering odds? Because he believed deeply in his God and loved Him above all things else. His was the compulsive conviction that to express his love for God, music was his best medium. So he gave to it his whole soul . . . all his heart. Being an authority on the Bible, naturally, his most sublime music is religious music. No single musical personality has so enriched the stream of inspirational, religious music as has this plodding, self-sacrificing God-lover—Johann Sebastian Bach. He set his own life as well as millions of others to music by putting a song in the soul.

Restoring the Lost Radiance

One of the greatest mission fields facing Christendom is the challenge to recapture the lost radiance of Christlike faith. Once it shone with bright illumination. Zest and fervor of a fresh, powerful witness penetrated darkness and dispelled it. But as the wheels of time rolled on and enthusiasms were absorbed by mundane things, part of the fresh, radiant winsomness was lost. In its place appeared dull, apathetic indifference—indifference that chills and kills. Without the lustre of life's radiance, the church will continue to stumble along with prim programs and easy answers while the world slips into totalitarianism by our default.

This is Christianity's worst foot forward. A dour and often sullen disposition is poor face for winning pagans. Poor, in that it mocks, and poor because it is dishonest representation of that Face which shone with victory as He overcame the world. Our wonder is that we win as many people to this cause as we do, not that we don't win more!

One of the great compliments Jesus paid His followers consisted of these words: "You are the light of the world." We are to be shining lights in a world of darkness; we ought to have an inner glow resulting from our relationship to the Source of light. Just as

116

the moon, having no light of its own, reflects the light of the sun, Christians are to be reflectors of the Source of light. No, Jesus did not say that you *have* the light, but that you *are* the light. Part of His real essence is in every man who is twice-born. But reflection is minimized by layers of dirt and dust which dull and dim brilliance. Many lives reflect so little amount of divine light because the love of the world has taken away their ability to illuminate.

Moses, after having been on the mountain in the presence of God, came down to the valley. The record says that he shone with an inexplicable radiance, but he knew it not. Whenever man has been in God's presence, it will show in his face and spirit, though the person is not conscious of what others are seeing. Real religion shows! That's it. Let there be no doubt about that fact. One can no more conceal the divine presence in him than he can conceal the footsteps of Satan when the evil one is permitted to trespass on the soul.

When confronted with the challenge to capture this historical encounter of Moses with God, Michaelangelo chiseled in marble and granite to no avail. How would a man carve out of stone the abstract virtue of radiance? It was hard enough to chisel the mighty form of Moses as a man. Finally, he decided to cut a pair of projecting horns out of stone in Moses' forehead so as to represent the emanating virtue of radiance. Divine endorsement spiraling from the heart and head of Moses spoke of God's indwelling presence.

Today as one stands before that work of a genius, there it is: radiant religion in solid stone pointing upward toward the face of God.

Joyful Religion

This I know: that if one's religion does not make his heart merry, his lips whistle, his heart rejoice and his mind reach out, it is not the religion of Jesus Christ. Religion that is freighted with sob-stories and funeral dirges, that majors on what is wrong with the world while overlooking the many things that are right, religion summed up in more don'ts than do's, one that

117

"harps" on what must be given up instead of what it is a privilege to take up, then call it what you will, but don't call it the religion of Jesus Christ! Such religion doesn't remotely resemble Christ-likeness.

Early Christendom absorbed much from mystic religions in the world about it. From the Essenes came asceticism. From Egyptian and Persian mystery religions came a pinch of this and a dash of that. After Jesus was no longer present with His disciples in the flesh, all sorts of superstition, myths, hearsay and old wives' tales crept in as partial testimony in individual experiences. With the passing of time, some of these alien accounts were glued to the pages of religious lore, while many people believed them as "gospel" truth. Perhaps none has dealt more lethal blows to the real truth than that killjoy, monastic type of self-effacement which parades today in pallid, puny witnessing. It demands death to all that is enjoyable as the price of religious dedication. What an absurd claim! How far can one miss the import of His teachings? True, there are many passions and ambitions that not only must be sub-limated but completely expelled if one is to be a good disciple of Jesus Christ. That relationship is no license to sin; such new-bought freedom is not a series of green lights through which a person speeds while hazarding the lives of other travelers. But to imply that Jesus was mostly death impulse in action is to con-tradict fact.

This is one reason why evangelists and evangelism often have failed to sound the real depths of spiritual significance. They have taken all the fun out of it! Contending that nearly everything that is enjoyable is either worldly or immoral, they leave no dimension in which abundant living can be experienced. Abundant is sub-stituted in their thinking for negation, narrowness, and morti-fication.

It is no wonder that droves of young people turn away from such demands. The damage done in the church and out by these well-intentioned, though misguided efforts is incalculable. It is a disconcerting but enlightening process to trace certain personal-ities in history who have climbed to power. Many once were mildly religious but either gave up religion because of disappointment in some other religionist, or failing to understand what the real message was, decided they could not fit into its claims. Stalin was once a candidate for the priesthood.

A modern reformation is needed to reclaim the lost radiance of Christian faith, a reformation that pursues the holy grail that is potential in this generation of young men and women whose lives count for but little. Joyful religion is real living.

When a superlative life approaches the time to die, much of the perennial freshness is maintained even in old age. Like ascending treads on a staircase, each year presents another step and riser in life's hierarchy of values and joys. Life should not be an inverted V where the climax of living was reached in middle age. Rather, it should be a vertical line pointing upward. The promise in the first Psalm is that the "Godly man shall be like a tree, planted by the rivers of water; that bringeth forth his fruit in season; his leaf also shall not wither; and whatsoever he doeth shall prosper."

Man's best guarantee that he shall live beyond the grave is that he has really lived on this side of the grave. No one will get in heaven until heaven first gets in him. So, eternal life is a present possession if it is to be a future possession. The sheen, harmony and radiance begun in this life continues in brighter lustre in the life to come.

"I believe it is the dullest book I've ever read," a lady remarked as she thrust it down in disgust. A few years later the same lady met the author of the dull book. There were many more meetings and she fell in love with the author. Under those conditions she reread the book. The second reading produced a different impression altogether. Why? Because love gives meaning to anything and anybody—meaning and significance that isn't *there* without love. Many of you who read these lines may consider life dull or as an unpleasant interruption of nothingness. Then cheer up—it can become a magnificent obsession. But not until you come to know and love the Author of Life.

119

Profiles

of 6

Greatness

It is not learning, grace nor gear,
Nor easy meat and drink,
But bitter pinch of pain and fear
That makes creation think.[1]

"He that is greatest among you shall be your servant."—Jesus Christ

EVERY NATION HAS a roster of personalities which it calls great: Israel her Solomons, Asia her Akbars and Tamerlanes, France her Hugos, Britain her Gladstones and Disraelis, Russia her Czars, Germany her Fredericks, Greece her Alexanders, Egypt her Ptolemys. Heroes and heroines walk across the pages of historical prose and poetry, leaving behind them a trail of ardent admirers and devotees. A close study of the nature of many of these so-called great personalities reveals a sordid story: many were scheming opportunists, tyrants, or egomaniacs; yet all sailed under the banners of championing the rights of common men or their downtrodden brothers.

Today the same old error is being repeated. Millions stand agog with admiration at twentieth-century would-be saviours on the international scene. Other idols—in sports, theatre, television—are held in near-holy admiration by their devoted admirers. We, like our predecessors, have our heroes—the persons whom we call great. In every profession there are those who ring the bells or who cut the stencils from which the rank and file run their copies. Umpires, referees, prototypes, these either impel or imperil the lives of the human race. The dangers involved are not in following a leader, but in failing to choose the right kind of leader to follow.

This fact necessitates the right answer to the question, Who are

[1] Rudyard Kipling, "The Benefactors." Stanza 3.

the great people in history? When each contender is stripped of his nationalism, is anything left in him which all nations can admire? What standards shall we lay alongside their lives to measure true greatness?

CONTEMPORARY STANDARDS OF GREATNESS

The Childish Estimate of Greatness: Material Things

> Ill fares the land to hastening ills a prey;
> When wealth accumulates, and men decay.[2]

The childish estimate of greatness consists in *things*: a nation or an individual is great if it possesses an abundance of material things which make for comfortable living, financial security, and freedom from enslaving manual labor. Stocks and bonds, cattle and cash, real estate and minerals, industries, rails, laboratories, looms and lathes are the components of greatness, according to the childish reasoning. And while these criteria are childish, nonetheless, this measurement is characteristic of most adults today. Mania for more is the identifying insignia for today's businessmen and women who are determined, not only to keep up with the Joneses, but want to pass them on a curve. Bigger and bigger, more and more are the driving whips of present-day leaders. Such values have become part and parcel of the American people. Men are measured in terms of their financial worth. Material, not spiritual or mental, wealth opens most doors of opportunity. It is Wall-Street gospel which says money will buy anything you want, including people. A price tag is on the head of every man—such is the belief of this school of earth-bound economists. As a result, the best years of the twenties, thirties and forties are nervously sacrificed for the fifties and sixties. When one can slow down and enjoy what has been earned at the expense of arduous toil, ofttimes ulcers, estrangement to church, family and God have robbed him of the capacity to enjoy. Hence, today's paradoxical predicament: youth

[2] Oliver Goldsmith, "The Deserted Village." Line 51.

121

with faculties for enjoyment but few facilities; age with facilities, but few or no faculties.

Actually, this estimate of greatness, which is justified only in the minds of worldlings, is a greater threat to world stability than the unmasked idolatry of communism's materialistic goals. In the final analysis they are much alike. Whereas communism contends man is nothing but matter in motion—motion which is regulated by economic determinism—capitalism has some rosy ideas and ideals, but in practice is little different from dialectic materialism on which Lenin and Marx based their central theory. Functionally, it is easy to see mammon rating a decidedly higher berth than God.

Travel wherever you will and you will find that most nations stand agog at America's many-splendored gadgets. Our automatic dishwashers, eggbeaters and percolators never cease to intrigue and arouse the envy of multimillions around the globe. Yet, despite their admiration and envy of our material things, the disconcerting impression is that few nations, if any, think that we are a great people! Now they rush to assure us that great individuals have been in the stream of American inventiveness all along and number many in today's American population, but taking us as a whole, they fail to see the distinctive features of genuine greatness amidst this conglomeration of things.

The hard-learned wisdom of history points an accusing finger at the growing worship of mammon. Goethe warns that a nation can endure anything except continuous prosperity. Viewing a British empire that sprawled all over the world in his day, Wordsworth was prompted to say,

> The world is too much with us; late and soon,
> Getting and spending, we lay waste our powers.[3]

Hear the words of Jesus: "A man's life consisteth not in the abundance of the things which he possesses." When all is said and done, the wisest will conclude that life is not measured by accumulation but by outlay, not by how much one has saved but how much he

[3] William Wordsworth, "The World Is Too Much With Us."

has wisely expended, not by distance traveled but by the route taken.

It is incumbent upon every Christian to cultivate a sensible attitude toward things. Admittedly, it is easier to work a miracle than it is to maintain a healthy, balanced attitude in this respect. It should be daily discipline to reassess the time taken, the thoughts invested and the plan formulated in pursuing economic well-being. Herein the example of Jesus Christ should be our clear direction. He warned against the habit of laying up treasures on earth where moth and rust corrupt and where thieves dig through and steal. He encouraged heavenly investments where none of the minus factors are present. But who can write a check on a heavenly depository in order to pay the rent when it comes due? That is why a balanced judgment must prevail in a Christian's life when it comes to sensible handling of money. The same admonishing voice, "Be not distracted about your life, what you shall eat, or drink, or for the body what you shall wear . . ." also endorsed individual initiative in investing, getting and reckoning the cost before beginning construction.

In the parable to illustrate the right attitude concerning things, Jesus made it clear that it wasn't Lazarus's poverty that placed him in Abraham's bosom any more than it was the wealth of Dives that sent him to Hades. The attitude of each determined his destiny. Somewhere between need and desire, between asceticism and indulgence, is the right place for a Christian to take a stand. Between an attitude that unconsciously envies those who possess many things while consciously pretending to place no importance on what is envied, on one hand, and an honest admission that things in their rightful place can be servants instead of masters, on the other hand, is hard-found ground.

In 1923 a group of the world's most successful financiers met at the Edgewater Beach Hotel in Chicago for their national convention. Among those present were the president of the largest independent steel company in the world, the greatest wheat speculator, and the president of the New York Stock Exchange. In addition, there were present a member of the President's cabinet, the greatest

123

"bear" on Wall Street, the president of the Bank of International Settlements, and the head of the world's greatest monopoly.

Twenty-five years later, a newspaper reporter traced the lives of those rich men to see how they turned out after a quarter of a century; how they died, and how they left their vast estates. His findings should make the shrewdest calculator stop cold in his tracks. The president of the steel company, Charles Schwab, lived on borrowed money the last five years of his life and died broke. The utility operator, Samuel Insull, died in virtual exile. Arthur Patton, the wheat speculator, died abroad, insolvent. The president of the Stock Exchange, Richard Whitney, had served a term in Sing Sing Prison. Albert Fall, the member of the President's cabinet, was pardoned from prison so he could die at home. The Wall Street "bear," Jesse Livermore, committed suicide. The head of the world's greatest monopoly, Ivar Krueger, committed suicide. Each of these men had learned how to make a living but failed to learn how to make a life. Now what demented mind would conclude that material wealth makes for greatness or happiness? No person is wealthy to whom the grave brings bankruptcy!

The Barbarian Estimate: Force

This second contemporary estimate of greatness comes from the barbarian mind. It contends that man is an animal—a fighting animal. So, the best fighter is the greatest animal. This is an oversimplification of the old Prussian position, the philosophy of Nietzsche, who would encourage belligerence, militancy and munitions. Greatness consists in brute force, either for a nation or an individual. Peace, kindness, "live and let live" philosophies, belong to weaklings. The only "gospel" worth believing is that which teaches survival of the fittest. If there is a God, they contend, then He is always on the side with the biggest battalions. Human virility is measured by one's ability to kill—kill to weed out from the human race the weaklings who will not kill others. As a storm twists and bends large trees and in the process removes dead limbs and twigs, so war is designed to remove the dead wood of humanity. In one form or another, this type of thinking has dominated the war departments of nations all the way back in recorded history.

If military strength exists as self-protection as well as protection for the weak who cannot defend themselves, then it is a crime to be militarily weak, especially in a world where barbarians are armed. The Old Testament prophets who spoke of beating the implements of war into plowshares and pruning hooks and of nations studying war no more, evidently didn't have the twentieth century in mind. As I write these lines, the biggest business in our world is how to kill efficiently. Yet modern man has so rationalized which conditions are defensive and which offensive that the picture has run together, making it even more difficult to know what part, if any, belongs to a child of God.

No strategy would better serve the ends of communism than for America to yield to a policy of pacifism—pacifism which merely enunciates high-sounding principles and ideals, parades with visionary banners, and cries to high heaven at the slightest rattle of a sword. Ideals we must have, higher even than those pacifists are raving about; but the other half of the story needs to be told too. What chance do either ideals or the idealists have in a world which would be taken over by fiends and brutal, low-browed murderers? In such a merciless world the only new things learned would be multiples of pain. The error of pacifists is failing to reconcile the ugly present reality with distant, hoped-for ideals. Accommodation, not compromise, sometimes can be an operative procedure, but falls short of a working policy when one side insists on calling all the plays.

There is equal danger in the other direction. To believe that God is on the side with the biggest battalions is to impute a cruel interpretation to the words and deeds of Jesus Christ. That belief would make of Him a sword-rattler, a perennial candidate for an army khaki or navy blue uniform, ever ready to give holy sanction to combat, defensive or otherwise. "The Lord is on our side," has been the impious claim of every army that marched into battle! The blunt truth is that God doesn't take sides; least of all, when men set themselves to the infamous business of killing one another.

Had the barbarian standard of greatness been valid, America would stand without a peer. Acres of war matériel deployed all over the face of the earth a decade and a half ago spoke of an endless

125

arsenal of weapons. Despite this mass assemblage of tanks, ships, guns and planes, less than twenty years later here we are in the same old business, though on a scale that makes the former look like a child's model. It could be expected that once a nation bows to the childish estimate of greatness, a logical sequel would be armed might, in order to protect things and all they represent.

The folly of this measurement is history's oldest error: one man clubbing another to death as recorded on chalk cliffs of antiquity. As a matter of fact, the first family yielded a son as murderer and the other son as the one murdered.

Few, if any, can comprehend the cost, in terms of things expended, to wage warfare. One senator has done some interesting arithmetic along this line. In the day of Caesar, according to the senator's calculations, it cost about seventy-five cents to kill a man. During Napoleonic wars, this price rose to about three thousand dollars per man. Then it climbed to five thousand dollars in the War Between the States in America. For each man killed in World War I, the cost was twenty-one thousand dollars. The Second World War cost the warring countries over fifty thousand dollars for each man killed! If one starts counting from the year 2000 B.C. and continues to count to the present time, he will find that humanity has enjoyed less than three hundred years of freedom from war. So war is not an unusual phenomenon; it is the most familiar activity among us. Peace has been little more than short intervals between wars, for enemy identification.

Yet, it seems almost vulgar to mention the cost of wars in terms of economics. Least of importance is the cost in dollars and cents. Who can estimate the tons of misery and grief? What scales can accurately weigh agony? Who replaces the bombed-out churches, hospitals, homes, schools? The death of hope and equity, the obliteration of innocence, the eradication of decency and mercy, these are the real price tags of barbarism.

The voice of the church of Jesus Christ is too muted on this Satanic measure of greatness. Why isn't there a united, concerted voice of condemnation on man's cleverly laid and highly financed plans to obliterate a good portion of the human race? Too often the fight for what is called right becomes a mad scramble for what is left! No, war is not inevitable and the thing that goes farthest toward making it so, is the conviction that it is inevitable. Any farmer knows that it is easier to stop a seed from growing than it is to kill poisonous weeds after they have started growing over the land. Why couldn't the same principle be applied to armed conflict?

> What did you pray at war, Soldier,
> What did you pray at war?
> I prayed that we might do the thing we have not done before;
> That we might mobilize for peace, nor mobilize in vain,
> Lest Christ and man be forced to climb stark Calvary again![4]

In lighter vein, this obvious truth was voiced by two American Indians in a foxhole on Saipan during World War II. "The way I figure," one said, "when they smoked the peace pipe in 1918, nobody inhaled."

Less than two months after an atomic bomb destroyed Hiroshima, I walked through those ghastly ashes with horror and awe, which produced the mixed emotions of nausea, tears and penitence. The spectre before my eyes looked like a scene created by a hundred Frankensteins for Dante's *Inferno*. But today, it is common knowledge among even junior high school students that the atomic bomb which destroyed nearly a hundred thousand people in Hiroshima in less than an hour was little more than a firecracker compared to the thermonuclear warheads, the like of which this nation alone has more than 50,000!

Today our objective scientists can talk in cold-blooded terminology about "mega-death" in which countless numbers would meet a sudden end. The ghastly business of mass destruction is on the agenda of a thousand seminars as though the human race, in neurotic contemplation of this horror, were impelled in hell's direction. Recently, the advantage of surprise nuclear knockout was the subject of detailed consideration by high-level scientists. In what they called "The Delicate Balance of Terror," their frightful

---

[4] Reprinted by permission of Dodd, Mead & Company from "Pilot Bails Out" by Don Blanding. Copyright 1943 by Don Blanding.

127

speculations contend, "that two major and similar hypothetical countries can inflict 100 million deaths on each other by an all-out attack on the other's population and secondly, that if either launches a surprise attack on the enemy's retaliatory force, it can destroy the high fraction of 90 per cent of it. Then the victim's counterblow against the aggressor's cities will amount to 10 per cent of what it might otherwise be, so that the retaliation will only inflict 10 million deaths on the aggressor." And on it goes! In the final chapter of this reasoning, Oscar Morgenstern concludes, "The most interesting things in science at present are done only if they are related to war and war preparations—society does not accept the desire for knowledge unless it is in some way tied to war." Then, under the heading, "Fascination of War," he contends, "War preparations are necessary in order to justify the deepest desire for human knowledge." These are the apocalyptic prophecies of this barbarian concept of greatness. Pray God, if this is the best we can do, then who is brash enough to believe that mankind is worth saving?

In the ultimate outreach of decent values, man must learn a better way of settling his disputes than killing. If a nation's claim to greatness consists in bombs and bullets, then man stands no higher than the beasts of the jungles. As a matter of fact, he doesn't stand as high; even the murderous Bengal tiger will kill only for his meal—not the whole tribe of antelopes or the entire primitive settlement of human beings. In God's museum of things that matter, there will be no swords nor medals, no military standards and falderal. Except, of course, the sword that pierced the side of the Nazarene and a scabbard drawn to defend that innocent One in Gethsemane's Garden. Nor will the niches of heaven be occupied by Genghis Kahn, Hannibal, Caesar, Alexander, or anonymous militarists. Their names are legion. The counters of the City Four-Square will display but few mementos of earth: a rusty spike or two, a crude manger, a splintery, botched cross, a briary, thorny crown, a small boy's lunch box, a seamless coat, an empty perfume bottle—just a few such things.

Before leaving the barbarian estimate of greatness, we should

ask how a conscientious Christian is to relate himself to military service and still be true to the commandment, "Thou shalt not kill"? How do you work up the ability to kill while knowing that it is wrong to kill? This difficult paradox I have had to face personally and while my solution leaves much to be desired, nonetheless, it is the best I can do in the light of all that I see and know. Caught in this crossfire of conflicting forces, a Christian is somewhat like a highway patrolman who sees a motorist speeding. In the process of catching him, the patrolman breaks the speed law too. He must do so in order to overtake and arrest the intentional speeder. Technically, both men broke the law. But the motives were altogether different. Speeding down the world's highways are demon-possessed men who care nothing about the safety for the rest of the traffic. If the free world must exceed the speed limit in order to overtake the menace to innocent life, then no alternative is left to us. But we should be triply sure who the innocent lives are, lest law and breaker of the law be one and the same.

THE GRECIAN ESTIMATE OF GREATNESS: INTELLECT

Admittedly, this measure far outdistances the preceding two standards. Man is a rational creature and placing the laurels of merit at the door of qualitative thinking is much nearer the real center than all gadgets and military armor combined. The zenith of Greek learning is one of the pinnacles of civilization. To say that greatness consists in the power of the intellect to know, to think, to choose, is a sort of greatness of its own. Few conquering nations have been able to project their culture across most of the strata of the world. For Grecian culture to last over two thousand years is distinction well worthy of acclaim. The best idiom of expression devised by man, the Greek language, the cultured art of abstract thought—these and countless others live until this day.

The Bible insists that learning be a part of religious experience. Of the nearly 1,200 chapters and sixty-six books which make up its canon, not one chapter encourages mental sloth or condones

129

ignorance. On the contrary, that record is replete with admonition, rebuke, exhortation to "Study to show thyself approved. . . ." And though many wonderful things were accomplished by unschooled people in the first few centuries after Christ, one wonders what course Christendom would have taken had its most vocal champion, Paul of Tarsus, not been a well-educated man! God never has been able to work His sovereign purpose through dullards who refuse to cultivate their minds. This fact in itself is all the justification needed for Christian education on a far wider scale than our present grasp. The Christian Church must give no quarter to that lazy attitude of mind toward worship—lazy in its refusal to find an alternative to sentimentalizing and emoting. We must

> Learn to live, and live to learn,
> Ignorance like a fire doth burn.[5]

A little learning in the church is still a dangerous thing!

But to conclude that intellect and intelligence represent the optimum value in greatness is to overlook history's recurring warning: just to know for the sake of knowing, knowledge as an end rather than a means to nobler ends, can be man's most vicious enemy. Why? Because it is possible to know much while believing little. There are scholars who are "ever learning but never coming to a knowledge of the truth." If the apex of greatness could be reached through learning, then Jesus should have been a professor. Every well-educated person knows something of the pride inherent in the fact of knowing.

Look, for instance, at the community of Phi Beta Kappas. Who teaches the Sunday school classes in America's churches? The best informed people? In some cases they do. In the majority of cases, they do not. Is it that learning has encouraged a self-granted immunity from duty and participation? Does possession of facts excuse the possessor from lifting his share of the human load?

The irony of this day is that the person most to be feared is not a farmer, nor a factory worker, not even a soldier, but a nuclear physicist who does not have God in his conscience—nuclear giants who are godless midgets!

[5] Bayard Taylor, "To My Daughter." Stanza 1.

Japan was among the most literate nations on earth during the 1940's. More people could read and write among her seventy millions than in any other country. This fact notwithstanding, modern history records no details of human horror more gruesome than those committed by the literate Japanese servicemen. The blunt fact is that they knew better, but knowing did not assure better acting! Nor for that matter, did the many with graduate degrees among Hitler's SS Elite Corps. They hardly lacked in formal education; they lacked in moral judgment and righteous concern! But with all their brilliant inventions and scientific know-how, they still gave the world Dauchau, Buchenwald, and allied chambers of torturous death.

No, despite man's desperate need for better education, to place the blue premium of optimum greatness on intelligence is to disregard the fact that God did not make academic excellence the means of man's salvation. If knowledge had been the way out of the woods, then ignorance should have been punished as crime, and Christ died unnecessarily. To the best schooled generation in human history, it must be said that in all its learning, it has not yet learned life's two most elemental lessons: namely, without God man can not; without man God will not.

GOD'S STANDARDS OF GREATNESS

> *In success to share one's principles with the people.*
> *In failure to live them out alone; to be incorruptible by riches or honors.*
> *Unchangeable by poverty, unmoved by perils or power;*
> *These I call the qualities of a great man*—Mencius

The divine measure of true greatness, while placing proper evaluation on material things, on sensible consideration for survival, and endorsing learning as being indispensable to human betterment, nonetheless, moves in an opposite direction when defining the ultimate values of life. What men have considered wisdom, God has regarded as foolishness.

131

When Jesus was asked who was greatest in His Kingdom, He answered in words that no philosopher would have used. To His ambitious, self-centered disciples He talked of humility, sacrifice and courage. These words struck them as foreign, much as they strike us. To their unaccustomed ears He said, "He that is greatest among you shall be your servant."

Greatness Consists in Giving Yourself Away

"He that would lose his life for my sake shall find it." This glorious truth is the wisdom of all ages compressed into one blessed sentence. Since God's prescription for genuine living revolves around the verb "to give" instead of "to get," then to give of oneself is a happy, though sometimes painful experience. Self-giving is our desperate need! So long as one is prosperous enough to pick up a checkbook and write out full payment for all his desires, he will not know the genuine joy of giving a part of the checkwriter.

This type of greatness is never self-conscious. Since motivation is its least concern, it goes ahead with a magnanimous spirit without being bothered by the merits of the one receiving his gifts. Nowhere did Jesus say that beggars were to have complete sociological case studies made of their backgrounds before receiving the coin of passersby. The real import is not whether the beggar is deserving but whether we can give freely. Being generous with money and miserly with self speaks not of greatness at all. Greatness of this dimension never needs the lash of coercion because it does not go "like the quarry slave at night, scourged to his dungeon"; rather, with certain step and unreluctant gait, it rushes to embrace the moment of truth in duty with sacred enthusiasm. Suffused with a sense of selflessness, no quarter is given to thinking about greatness. It remembers the arresting judgment of Seneca, "A test of every man's character is how he takes praise." Praise or slander evoke relatively the same emotional reaction. This sort of thing is not taught, it is caught—caught like a contagion of spirit.

If self-giving is to be without alloy, it must generously admit that life, when surrendered to God through Christ, is expendable from

132

the first act of commitment. And while temperance and good sense must interplay, neither of these must sully or stifle the risks which faith demands. Far more important than life itself is the way of life, and in its defense and propagation individual life is often expended. But who shall raise the pagan criterion by reasoning that such expendability is waste? Not so! For this purpose life was made; to this end the child of God committed himself. Ultimate reality lies not in the candle nor the candle's flame but in the burning. So with life in God. Though the workman be lost, the work goes on in unbroken continuity.

Self-giving: no other action exceeds self-giving in the needs of the household of faith. This family of God has grown selfish—selfish to the core. Motivation for service needs to come in for a brisk, clean scrubbing. Once and for all, the church needs to shuck off its red, white, and blue contests, its door-prize techniques, its "you-will-get-this-out-of-it—if-you-will-do-thus-and-so" promises, its detailed descriptions of cushions instead of activity in surveying the dimensions of crosses. All of these need to be replaced by a forthright challenge to give of self and substance with no expectation of return. Then, and only then, can there be valid, spiritual return. Greatness of God's design never asks, What do I get out of it?

Greatness Is in Responding to the Hard Places of Life With No Sense of Nobility, Since in Obedience to the Will of God One Could Not Do Otherwise

The unbroken treck of surrendered saints down through the centuries attest to this standard of value. A march of anonymous men has led through jungles, deserts, mountains and the paths of the sea, blazing new trails for God. They have braved every imaginable adverse condition so they could tell the good news to a lost world. Most of these places have been in hard environments, exacting severe toll of health, energy and spirit. Sometimes geography was almost as rough an issue as pagan idolatry. Both were encountered. Yet that granitic dedication in the hearts of God's pioneers was able to win out over the roughest odds. They, like many a flower, were "born to blush unseen and waste . . . [their]

133

sweetness on the desert air."[6] Scattered, perhaps—but not wasted. It is impossible for the sweetest fragrance of human sacrifice to be wasted when it is scattered in the cause of Christ for the good of mankind and the glory of God. Every such semblance of devotional aroma is intercepted by the nostrils of God from the desert air.

"But aren't you disappointed by now?" I asked the Franciscan Priest who had spent twenty-three years in the little Japanese village of Akaoka. "You say that you have been here that long and have only nine converts to Christianity?" He looked at me as though I had wounded him. "Don't say 'only nine,'" he rebuked, "say 'nine!'" I quickly drew back my typical, American activistic emphasis on numbers while he spoke in hushed, sacred tones much as he would repeat a litany of praise, about the lives and interests of the nine Japanese converts. After I had unloaded rations of food and personal items which these men, gaunt from malnutrition, had not seen for years, my mind wandered as it followed my searching eyes. There was little or nothing by way of material convenience and comfort; geography and climate in that part of the country, most of the year, is one cruel rampage after another. So, I thought what on earth is it that would cause three religious men to give their lives in this little, God-forsaken spot? The answer crashed down about me: there is nothing on earth that would cause them to do it. There is plenty in heaven, in God, which compels them to do it.

In a sense, these men, like countless others, were buried alive. Having died to their own desires and ambitions, they presented a resurrected soul, shaming my eager, easy, mundanely critical ego. The world call this nonsense, foolishness, fanaticism. God has a different name for it.

A ministerial friend in the deep South presents a contrast to my Japanese friends. After serving a few years in a small village church, he stripped his speech of every trace of constraint so far as talking about his ambitions was concerned. Quite frankly he admitted that he didn't have any time to waste, "to fool around" were his exact words, with a little church. "No two-by-four church

[6] Thomas Grey, "Elegy in a Country Churchyard."

for me," he arrogantly concluded. When asked for a definition of a "two-by-four church," he used the chance to describe, in long detail, all his pent-up disdain for things on a small scale, for simple, colorless people who refuse the shallow honor of sophistication. He wanted to be in the limelight, where things were happening; he wanted to know the boys in the upstairs rooms, "the brass," among whom decisions were made that affected the life-flow of the churches.

I had a hard time trying to choke down the dozen or so sermons that were begging to come out of me right about then. But I had to face the near-nauseating fact: this young preacher is a product of this day and age; what he believes and what he has learned have come from some kind of teachers. Has the older generation given rise to this line? Indeed it has. Do not pulpit committees and the congregations they represent often rate churches in terms of numerical size, big budgets and social prestige? Is there not an age-cycle idolatry behind most of the decisive plays within every denominational hierarchy? One would get the impression that until a minister is thirty-three he doesn't know the alphabet and after he gets to be forty-three, he has forgotten the multiplication table! So my young ministerial friend was just a bit brasher in his vocality than the rank and file of laymen who have created a climate in which that young parson thought such a sense of values was necessary or desirable.

This disconcerting dilemma prompted one keen thinker to demand a fifth freedom. Contending that the four basic freedoms about which we talk in America are not sufficient, he begged for a fifth one: the freedom from the necessity of being a big-shot! A needed freedom to be sure. Trying to be a big-shot is ignoble enough, but feeling that it is necessary is too much transgression.

When God speaks we have no alternative to saying, "Here am I Lord, send me. Send me anywhere You like, just be sure You are with me." This is greatness.

*Divine Greatness Is Seen When a Child of God Refuses to
Sit Astride the Moral Fence Until He Can Jump off on the
Side With the Biggest Crowds*

Cool calculation that weighs all the odds before taking a stand
speaks of no divinely wrought genuineness. It is after the odds
have been considered, costs counted, and the hazardous mission
fully surveyed that a great soul moves forward with courageous
initiative. Daring disciples have charted unknown worlds, doing
what was considered impossible by lesser breeds without the law.
Let there be no fear when others are quick to brand fearlessness
with the usual labels: "radical," "liberal," "fanatic." These become
insignia of noble identity. "So persecuted they the saints who were
before you." Talking about apostolic succession, this perhaps is
the only authentic criterion: whether or not one is in the stream
of successive persecution for the sake of Jesus of Nazareth. What
matters the name-calling? A price is paid for everything and sometimes the price for stalwart courage is your neck. Remembering
another's neck that was voluntarily extended and crucified makes
our submission more meaningful.

What right does a Christian have to be on a fence in the first
place? Every moral issue demands taking sides and there are but
two sides to take: the right one and the wrong one. Those who
scramble up the fence of rationalizing between the right and wrong
position merely call attention to their hypocrisy. Jesus was no
fence-sitter. Not one person got the idea that He could prepare a
diplomatic statement that would satisfy both sides on a crucial
issue. He didn't permit the tongue of discretion in the cheek of
propriety. Never! Always His knees were firm and refused to
buckle under when the going got rough. Today as we face a
blistering barrage of criticism, carping insults and vulgar invective,
when old systems crumble before our eyes, let us measure up.
Never before has there been such an acid test of Christian religion
as this day. Ours is a magnificent chance to show the big dimensions of our God, His Christ and the transforming dimensions
and powers of Christian faith. Any type of abiding qualitative

136

greatness among humans must be some sort of imitation of God's greatness. Apart from this, ours is cheap theatrics, utter sham and play-acting. "He that is greatest among you shall be your servant."

This, then, in part, is the anatomy of genuine greatness. Obviously, I have had to speak solely from observation of others on this subject. In the words of William Makepeace Thackeray: "To endure is greater than to dare; to tire out hostile fortune; to be daunted by no difficulty; to keep heart when all have lost it; to go through intrigue spotless; to forego even ambition when the end is gained—who can say this is not greatness?"[7]

[7] *The Virginians*, Chapter 92.

When Religion Gets You in Trouble

7

"All who will live godly, in Christ Jesus shall suffer persecution."—Paul the Apostle

"Woe unto you when all men speak well of you."—Jesus Christ

THERE IS LITTLE wonder they crucified Jesus. A placid world lulled to sleep by conventionalism, protocol and platitudes had no mind nor mood for such a revolutionary as Jesus of Nazareth. His impact was more like a whirlwind in a dust bowl than a gentle zephyr. Many religionists of His day had permitted their religious interests to degenerate into cunning, self-interests. Accepting cruelties and inequities either as God-ordained, or fate's inevitability, they waited for public sentiment, followed lines of least resistance, sought creature comforts at the expense of holier things, and died weaklings. To these people Jesus was a magnificent disturbance. And He has been disturbing such indifference ever since. His religion got Him in trouble—just as the same faith will assure trouble today when profession and practice are one. To him who dares apply his religion to everyday living, one thing is certain: trouble.

WHY RELIGIOUS TROUBLE IS INEVITABLE

Christian Faith's Refusal to Compromise With Paganism

The nature of Christian faith is explosive, fermentive, status-changing. Demanding action, it cannot be contained in a vacuum of inertia. Paganism thrives in complacency, alienation, and self-satisfaction. When these two forces meet, conflict is inevitable.

138

Co-existence is out of the question: one will ultimately reign as victor over the other. The demand for compromise is a demand of death to faith's potency. Knowing this, Christian faith runs the risk of being dogmatic to maintain its undefiled purity and its undiluted potency.

That such conflict is inevitable is seen in the words of Jesus addressed to the early disciples whom He sent out as witnesses. Matthew states the case. They were to go out as sheep in the midst of wolves. He warned them to anticipate a negative response in many places. The pay-off for their courageous initiative was to be persecution, arrest, imprisonment, ridicule and sometimes death. In the process they were to guard against belligerence and vindictiveness. To be wise as serpents and harmless as doves was a big order for these simple, willing people. It is amazing that their courage held as firmly as it did, what with all the odds stacked against their chances of succeeding. To the modern disciple whose basic premise in reasoning is to ask, "What do I get out of it?" the compensation sounds off-beat. He promised them that they would get in trouble, that they would suffer much, that persecution would surely trail their steps, but in the process if they remained faithful they would be saved. Salvation! Is that all? That was enough to those hardy souls who knew what salvation involved.

He left no doubt about the fact that they would get in trouble if they lived up to the requirements of their faith. The conflict of truth with error, rightness with evil, would produce painful friction. Father would be set against son and daughter against mother. Within the same household a division would arise as a result of the new way of life in Him.

Before we proceed further with this consideration of religious trouble, let it be honestly admitted that all trouble which comes to Christians is not an asset to their Lord or themselves. Trouble, its nature and cause must be clearly delineated if the Kingdom is to be credited or discredited. It is quite easy to rationalize by saying that emotional pronouncements, immature judgments and unregenerate initiative is part and parcel of being an active Christian. Much of the trouble in the household of faith obviously results not from courageous, intelligent identification with Christlike devotion, but from intemperance, foolhardiness, egotism, lack of restraint, or contamination by evil's allure. Trying to squeeze some theological asset out of these twisted tubes is wasted effort. Ignorance, fanaticism, ill judgment have a way of producing all sorts of headaches and heartaches in religious service, but to call them the inevitable consequences of discipleship is to misrepresent the facts. Diotrophes still loves to have pre-eminence among the brethren and all the brethren don't like him to be pre-eminent! Confusion, division, ill spirits often ensue. The blessings inherent in the beatitude belong to those about whom men speak all manner of evil *falsely*—not the evil which is accurately reported. If men speak ill of us, the alternative is to live so that nobody will believe them. No, some of the trouble annexed to religious living is neither the result of intelligent discipleship nor a compliment to the Christ so inadequately represented by the effort.

Jesus was talking about adverse reaction to courageous commitment. This is a different sort of trouble. Business crises resulting from one's refusal to be a party to crooked dealings; ridicule appendaged to championing unpopular causes; slander issuing from hateful lips because a Christian could not be bought or made to buckle under—these are the components of genuine trouble. This is the kind of predicament from which real character is made. Divisions that grow out of honest convictions, loneliness which haunts life because of being separated from worldly companions, duty done to the accompaniment of Caesar's hecklers, are positive proof that the disciple is following in the footsteps of his Master.

When Jesus spelled out the nature of human response, making sure that His disciples understood what they were getting into, it is a compliment to them that they did not flee in the face of such awesome prospects. They were to witness with the Holy Spirit as their companion. The indwelling presence of the Father would offset the persecutive pressures of paganism. Like the eye in the midst of a storm, they were to live in relative tranquility amidst turbulence and social strife. Theirs was a dual citizenship: two worlds—one foot on earth, the other in heaven; they were creatures of time but heirs of eternity. They were the losers of battles but the winners of wars.

At every hand, temptation presented itself to compromise or at least to accommodate Christian faith to rampant paganism. Had early Christians yielded to this incessant barrage, the new, young faith would have been swallowed up in a desert of mystery religions. The two ways of life were, and are, antithetic. Any effort at synthesis results in a poor substitute for the genuine edition. This early dynamic stood its ground against unbelievable odds and then took the initiative, primarily because of the impetus provided by the Holy Spirit. Its strategy was a grand offensive. Verbs that speak of militant action were on Christian lips: go, tell, stand fast, be of good cheer, believe, love, lift, sing, pray, give—these became the fibre of their strength, compelling them onward until the pagan empire of Rome began to disintegrate and crumble to dust.

Midway of this twentieth century it is difficult to find a parallel to their consummate zeal. Instead, ours is a tame, powerless ethic, so devoid of that revolutionary momentum that shook the gates of prisons and released their godly inmates. Too many prophets have acquiesced in the role of priests. It is becoming easier all the while to condemn evil only in the abstract. All Goliaths have not been slain, so where are the Davids with ready slings in hand? John the Baptist still is needed to declare that it is not lawful for a man to live with another's wife. The forthright severity of an olden prophet needs to look our guilty world straight in the eye and say, "Thou art the man." To every despotic Pharaoh should be proclaimed, "Let my people go." When faith is genuine, it will summon the fortitude so to declare.

Jesus the Great Disturber

"When the fight begins within himself, a man is worth something," Browning reminds. The strange words of Jesus, "I came not to bring peace but a sword," aroused in many that old militant hunger to throw out the Roman army of occupation. Initial hearing of these words revived hopes of a coming Messiah who would establish an earthly kingdom with headquarters in Jerusalem. A

141

kingdom involving troops, marching parades, military arsenals and the falderal belonging to such approaches. What did Jesus mean—this man of tranquility, the Prince of Peace, the very One who rebuked Peter when he severed the ear from the servant of the high priest, warning, "He that takes the sword shall die by the sword"; "I came not to bring peace but a sword"? What kind of sword?

Disappointment swept over His disciples when He made it clear that the sword about which He spoke had not steel in it. His battle-field was in the realm of the human spirit, and His strategy was based on love and compassion. There is a very definite sense in which He brought peace. Peace of heart, peace of purpose, peace in hope; a peace that is unsurpassed, qualitative, abiding; trans-cending peace occasioned by singleness of purpose. Peace annexed to enslavement in a holy cause; serenity which prevails when one abandons fear, anxiety and distraction. Yes, this is rare virtue, supplied from one exclusive source: loving allegiance to God. This possession, rarer than radium, is an unknown quotient to the un-regenerate world.

But peace to the people of Palestine meant little more than ces-sation from armed conflict. Even then, they knew little about soul serenity which holds in proper perspective material considerations and eternal verities.

Millions have cast Jesus in the role of a meek, benign pacifist. Contending that His words about swords, cleansing the temple, separating families where members are intentional pagans, are but accretions—additions to the records by later Christians—they try to justify their militant tendencies. A pale, effete ascetic fits their conceptions of Christ far more conveniently than a virile, muscular Galilean. Never is He more erroneously represented than by such distortion. In a definite way He brought a sword, a two-edged sword with a cutting edge of wisdom. A sword slicing through the crusts of falsehood, phonies and meanness, lays bare the heart of the matter. This is the dividing weapon between the temporal and eternal, the imitation and genuine. He was not the "big" man with a crusade in life, severing heads which impeded His progress;

instead He used a sword that disturbed lethargy and indifference, a sword which became a prophetic voice warning against monopolies and inequities which God will judge. His was a sword which demanded fair play and honest action for the weak and oppressed. Making clear that God cannot bless the oppressed and the oppressor at the same time, He encouraged the potential saint in every man, while condemning the sin in every man.

To illustrate this revolutionary teaching, He told two parables. Warning against taking a piece of unshrunken cloth to patch an old garment, Jesus cited how new cloth would shrink and in so doing the thread would pull out of the old garment, leaving a bigger hole than it covered. Just so with the new drawing power of His life-changing faith. He was saying that you cannot patch up an old life with a little dab of new religion and expect anything better than poor patchwork. When the real test comes and the tensions of an unregenerate life demand allegiance at one altar, while the tensions of God require allegiance at another, the result will be a tear—the old garment cannot stand the strain and the end product is in worse condition than before.

Wine business thrived in early Palestine, so Christ's reference to wineskins and fermentation found ready ears. In effect, He told them that they could not take the new wine of spiritual truth and pour it in old goatskin flasks which were dried in the parching sun. When the new wine began its fermentation, the old oilless skins would stretch, then split—wine and skin both would be lost. In like manner, when the dynamic of divine love is placed within the human spirit, something must give. Deep inside things will happen. No, Christian experience is not a whitewash job. It is more than reformation, or merely cleaning up sinful personality. It is new birth—in a word, it is new wine in new wineskins—so that the dimensions demanded by love's transformation can readily respond and contain. This was not just something else, some other religion, some modification of the old systems. It was uniquely its own— new from start to finish.

Not even domestic relations escaped this cutting sword. Where a pagan father thwarted the efforts of a mother who would follow

Christ, the sword made that strife possible. Sons and daughters, brothers and sisters, husbands and wives felt the sharp edge of truth's dissecting sword. Yes, He was a rude intrusion to their way of living, just as He is today. The status quo got little comfort from this disturber of their peace, this God-inflamed zealot who was determined to turn the world right side up! To have left Him alone would have meant death to their way of life. Such a new, clean power would have swept through their foul souls like fire in dry grass. To ignore Him would have been as futile as saying that they did not need air to breathe. This they could not do. So, trouble came. It came when hate took the vicious allies of envy, jealousy, wounded pride, professional sterility, political intrigue and religious callousness, and compounded them into one final, thorough stroke: a cross!

Religious Trouble Was Inevitable Because Christian Faith Demanded That Its Followers Be Unadjusted Personalities

The strange folk who were called Christ-ians presented embarrassing contrasts to the pagan rabble. They were like a mirror held up in which the ugly face of sin's realism could be seen. And the pagans didn't like it. Many were unconscious of their low estate until this high plateau of clean living was practiced in their midst. Like the black man in Africa who, when he first saw a white man, asked for a mirror. That was the first time he knew he was black. Here were people in a barren country acting like millionaires, though most were penniless. They were suffused with a hope, while their status in society was little more than menial servitude. While men and women who knew not the Nazarene were resigned to fatalism, these Christ-followers were consumed by a contagious enthusiasm.

Their first lesson consisted in the fact that they could not live up to the stringent requirements of their leader if they did not walk differently from the unsaved. Their firsthand experience with Jesus left little room in their lives for laxity and carelessness. Because theirs was a creative, gripping tension which found expression through joyous telling of the good news, outsiders called them

144

"fools." Fools because they refused to conform. When sinners piped the tune, they refused to dance. What a compliment! What superb wisdom!

This type of person generally gets in trouble since the opposite sort equates devotion with dullness. The straight-living Christian is a plumb line beside the crooked nature of a non-Christian. Hence, contact generates friction which is common stock today.

Yet, one of modern man's biggest needs is to get involved, to get in trouble for God's sake. Christians stand in too well with the world; so much so, in fact, that it is often hard to distinguish them from non-Christians. The world can't see enough difference between us!

Part of this condition is caused by the craze to conform. No disease has reached epidemic stage among the American family as has the contagious "me-too-itus." Especially among the younger generation there is a deadly conformity to the same old patterns: a subservient ditto to the old slick traditions. "Make mine the same" isn't exactly the easygoing agreeableness it appears to be; instead, it may be monotonous rote of having no alternatives. Imitation, pirating, plagiarism—all are well-known processes in our day. Our loss of individuality is greater than our loss of national prestige. Is it a crime to be different? To think? To vote "no" when everyone seems to vote "yes"? Who killed the spirit of individuality?

Look at the nauseating evidence: subdivisions of houses, like a child's roughly hewn blocks stacked in unsightly rows; songs that begin where the latest hit parade left off; books that ride the same vulgar horses in phraseology and moral; clothes cut by assembly-line yardsticks; political jargon that mouths identical, meaningless platitudes; attitudes which allow no fresh wind to blow in; little, if any, creative, honest, soul-searching initiative. One of the obsessions of this society is the desire to fit in, to be liked at any price. No fate befalls it half so devastating as to be ignored. This is a revised version of a secular "gospel" which speaks of no good to come. It is hard to find a true individualist whose corners of creativity and unapologetic freedom have not been rounded off by the sanding belts of conformity. A hue and cry to "be like us" is as

145

incessant as a pneumatic drill. As people yield to its driveling absorption, a menace of mediocrity is turned loose to stalk our kind.

Little wonder so few good artists, writers, or musicians are produced in this climate. A good student of any of these disciplines usually is regarded with a jaundiced eye of envy, suspicion or distrust. This appalling state of things has come about largely by the surrender of our souls to the conformist gods of materialism, secularism and humanism. Little heroic sacrifice is required to be another unit of labor. For one to step out of line to be a person instead of being "people" might offend some weaker soul who never had a spark of creativity in him in the first place. Magnificent volunteers for the hard tasks of life are exhibition pieces today. Let someone shout from the housetops that no job is small when a big person does it! Big jobs requiring tall-standing souls who are willing to deviate from Madison Avenue methods challenge the best we have to offer. One thing is certain and sure: the world will never be transformed by men who say, "Make mine the same."

This conformist gospel has its own beatitudes: Blessed is the well-rounded for he shall be liked by all. Blessed is the man who never has a creative thought but always plays it safely by the accepted rules and the standards of orthodoxy. Well-rounded! But like a rubber ball, the well-rounded person is apt to roll with the slightest push in any direction.

They thought Jesus a "square" just because He wouldn't roll with the crowd. Because the "square" stood His ground, He inspired such warning words as

> Better like Hector in the field to die,
> Than like a perfumed Paris turn and fly.[1]

The conformist voice is more out of place, yet more in evidence, in the Christian Church than anywhere else. "It was good for Paul and Silas, and it's good enough for me," may or may not be a timely compliment. Instead of proclaiming, "Be not conformed to this world but be ye transformed," the church too often has emoted and sentimentalized about peace, security, happiness, love and easy

[1] Henry W. Longfellow, "Morituri Salutamus," stanza 10.

virtues. Conforming to the world is not only accepted in many places but expected. Now the time has come to change the tune: the message of the church of Jesus Christ is to be a part of the world's solution, not a part of the problem. The blind cannot lead the blind without both inevitably falling in the ditch.

The trouble comes when a dedicated Christian tries to remain a human being amidst all sorts of stereotyped, pressurized propaganda. Penalties are ruthless and severe for the singular soul who insists that devotion to his Lord and domination does not require becoming a blob of ditto marks to all who equate human opinion with divine authority. When cooperation requires selling one's soul, then cooperation is idolatry. Parading under the guise of orthodoxy, this denuding force which would reduce every life to the same common, sectarian denominator, is growing like a behemoth in many of the major denominations. Let a fresh voice be heard and instantly the watchdogs of orthodoxy are alerted to bark and sniff as though heresy had already threatened the ramparts which they feel are exclusively theirs to watch. While piously condemning totalitarianism in its political-economic expression, they gladly embrace it in ecclesiastical form with no sense of shame or feeling of contradiction.

The penalties for failing to go along with the "powers that be" are often as insidious as they are varied. Being ignored when the honors are passed out, being shunted to the sidelines when consideration for strategic service is the issue, being shut out by the wink of endorsement to the other fellow or by the nod of assent which ruptures one's chance for promotion—these are but a few of the ways in which individualists are penalized for the crime of remaining human beings.

Perhaps no force has contributed more to the present climate of diluted integrity than this loss of personal identity. Basic honesty is involved and when one rationalizes that there is a truthful way to lie, and honest way to steal and a respectable way to degrade life, then little is required to make such a person a rubber stamp of conformity.

Most of the temptations of Jesus added up to this same kind of

147

pressure. Blend into contemporary environment, be well-adjusted, fit in, be likable, accommodate the desires of the "good" people, compromise starchy ideals with the more practical, workable necessities of realism—all these He steadfastly refused to do. So they killed Him. Trouble? Indeed there is, when respect for individuality is given precedence over a mimeographed copy of some other person's life. If this be true, then no need is greater in Christendom than the need of a lot of honest trouble!

Religious Trouble Is Inevitable Because Christianity Demands a United Witness in a Divided World

When Jesus knelt and prayed, "O Father, I pray that they all may be one," was He asking for oneness of spirit, unity of organization, singleness of purpose, or what? The present predicament of Christendom contradicts these measures of oneness. There is neither unity of organization nor of spirit, while there is plenty of room for diversity of spiritual purpose. Paul's exhortation in Ephesians, "Endeavor to keep the unity of the spirit in the bond of peace," is seldom heeded by kingdom individuals who insist that solo effort is to be desired above a chorus.

Let us admit it: there is little or no sense of oneness either in our methods or motives. Each pursues his own private "revelations" with little regard for the well-being of others. Much of the trouble of the kingdom comes in at this point. Some believe the millenneum would suddenly appear if the major denominations would merge into one monolithic structure. Evidently history's hand-learned wisdom is never consulted by such ardent enthusiasts. While there can be close cooperative efforts among all the branches of Christendom, the real need is not so much a matter of organic unity as unity of spirit and purpose. The wedges of suspicion and sectarian pride, the cleavages of ecclesiastical snobbishness, the crevices of exclusiveness—these are the curses and contradictions of the cause. These engender trouble when one tries to remember that God has other sheep which we know nothing about.

The "election" complex has cursed many a nation by encouraging an erroneous belief that one group has certain priorities with God and therefore can dispense divine favor at will. This is the infamous line which led to the inquisition, the Massacre of St. Bartholomew, to the schism which tore asunder the fabric of the household of faith. We shall never be able to outthink, outlive, and outsmart the Marxists until we rid every communion in Christendom of the methods and motives which created the climate for communism's advent and growth. Each community must be an experiment in practical Christianity, proving to the world that we have something in the sacrificial life of Christ which is not remotely offered in any other way of life. It will be a happy day for the world when Christians are all at least on speaking terms with each other. Maybe then the idea of brotherhood would get an honest hearing.

One day I stood on the rocky coast watching the tide go out. As it receded, sharp, craggy rocks with little suction holes held puddles of sea water captive. A hot sun bore down on the small, isolated holes of water changing them to warm, insipid puddles. But it was not long before the tide returned, fresh and forceful. It engulfed each tiny puddle into one foaming force. Sometimes it looks as though our hundreds of religious sects and cults, like the isolated puddles of sea water, stand aloof with a jaundiced eye of suspicion and envy of one another. What is needed is a tidal wave of God's love to engulf our narrow dimensions and swallow us up in the broader dimensions of divine love. It is a singular tragedy that while this world is divided into many camps, classes and castes, that the one major force which should demand unity of spirit—the church—merely adds to the divisiveness!

There is but one true church—the ecclesia—the "called out of the world" persons, the redeemed, the regenerate, the twice-born. But some of this type is in all communions of Christian faith. No one organized group comprises it, no one race, or creed, all the claims of religious monopolists notwithstanding. From the four corners of the earth come the godly to populate His Kingdom. The keys of the Kingdom are given today, as originally, to the sons of the Kingdom whose nature is fashioned after Christ's nature. This is a prerogative of divine favor, not of historical vantage. When a child of God gets in trouble because of his efforts to love all God's children, then glory be! He is never more of a compliment to his Christ.

149

Trouble Is Inevitable Since Christian Faith Demands That Love Be Implemented

Love has a proclivity for getting involved. Never content to lie dormant or take the object of its affection for granted, love will find a way to express its load of concern. This wondrous life-force called love is the only thing in existence that the more of it you give away, the more of it you have. It is the only service which power cannot command and money cannot buy.

When we set ourselves to the privilege of loving the sinner while hating his sin, it requires more wisdom than many possess to distinguish the two processes. To isolate sinful deed and spirit without leaving the wrong impression on the one in whose life the sin exists is tricky business. Yet, it is the main job assigned to every true child of the King. Most ministers will admit that it is easier to charge ther homiletical batteries on sermons which deal with the subject of hell than those which chart the dimensions of heaven. Denunciation comes twice as easily as positive affirmation.

At least this was the impression left on a congregation and its pulpit committee recently. Two preachers were invited to speak to the congregation. The first minister preached on hell. His words were threatening, his spirit negative and his whole demeanor seemed to enhance his subject. But the experience left the congregation cold and flat. They unanimously concluded that He was not God's man for their congregation. But the second preacher chose the same subject for his sermon. He boldly spoke of hell's reality, of the conditions which make it necessary and the routes of human living which lead down. The congregation unanimously called the second preacher as their pastor. When asked why since both men preached on "hell," they answered, "The first man left the impression that most would be going to hell and that he wasn't too unhappy about the fact. But the second man left the impression that he was sorry, deep inside, that anyone would so miss the purpose of God and go to hell." Such is the quality of love's implementation—in preaching and in practice.

Mrs. Adams was called the weakest woman in our neighborhood. Weak, because she continued to live with a worthless husband who failed to provide her the basic necessities, a man whose badge of identity was a bottle and debts. Years of misery were her lot as she quietly accepted the cruelties of critical neighbors and her tyrannical husband. Often he would come home at two o'clock in the morning, staggering in his drunkenness, and demand that she get up and cook him something to eat. Bounding to her feet, she would go out the back door in the cold of night, cut enough wood to fire the cheap, cast-iron stove, and bake bread for the worthless man. One day my mother asked her, "How is it that you continue to live with Sam? He never says a kind word to you, never treats you even as a human being." Never shall I forget that straight-forward,, telling reply. "You see, Mrs. McClain, it's like this: I love him." That's all she said. That was enough. I know of nothing else on earth which would have held together that good woman and her evil man. No, she never won him to her Christ who taught her to love even the unlovely. I wish I could make this illustration more dramatic by saying that her persevering love won him in the end, but so to state would be dishonest. He died drunk one night, in the same stupor, filth, and sorriness in which he lived. But she won something more valuable than a man to sobriety: she won a place in the hearts of impatient, loveless folks by her selfless example of implementing love by lovely action. If just a bit of all the talk, the songs and sonnets about love were translated into deeds, ours would be a kinder, less miserable world. There was no doubt left about what constitutes the core of real religion when Jesus summed it all up: loving God with all that is in us and loving our neighbors as well as we love ourselves—this covered the whole field of human endeavor.

If faith commands love to take the initiative in reconciliation and one party refuses to be reconciled, then the friction and trouble which usually ensues is a compliment to the love-propelled initiator. When love turns its other cheek and a heavy hand smites it, then wear the black eye with esteem, esteem unakin to intentional martyrdom. When walking life's rock-pitted second miles gets us involved in all sorts of tangles, so what? This is the nature of the promise; this is the genius of Christian experience.

It was a love affair which caused the crucifixion on Calvary! God

151

loving the world with such ardor that His only Son was given to redeem the unlovely.

Could we with ink the ocean fill, and were the sky of parchment made,
Were every stick on earth a quill and every man a scribe by trade,
To write the love of God above, would drain the ocean dry,
Nor could the scroll contain the whole, though stretched from sky to sky.[2]

THE TYPE OF TROUBLE RELIGION CAUSES

Economic Trouble

One historian has concluded that all wars are fought between the "haves" and the "have-nots." The so-called ideological struggles of the twentieth century still are being waged over meat and bread, stocks and bonds, and the keys to universal resources. Christian religion must take an honest look at the world of economics, of finances, fiscal injustices, monopolies, graft, greed, and starvation. If the church of Jesus Christ has nothing to say about this predicament—no strong authoritative warning against such injustice—then it has no right to speak at all! We have failed to insist that the shadow of the cross should fall across every churchman's pocketbook. In all the talk about baptism, why not insist that the pocketbook—or the attitude it represents—be immersed too? There are enough people belonging to churches and synagogues to change the whole picture of world finance, if they would but live according to God's mandates in the matter of economics.

Nothing explains our having to render to Caesar the lion's share better than the fact that we have failed to render to Christ the things which are His. Caesar is getting both shares. Woe to that minister, however, who proclaims, in searching severity, God's holy injunctions! He had better watch out: trouble inevitably sparks from such timely truth. Members who will snore through his preaching on social justice, new birth, Christian education, and so forth, will suddenly jump awake the minute he mentions money. Little wonder that so many churches are in financial trouble: they

[2] These lines are said to have been penciled on the wall of a narrow room of an asylum by a man suffering from mental illness.

are guilty of the sin of miserliness, of cheating God by failing to give what is required under law, to say nothing about what grace would generously yield. How long will we have to plod, borrow, skimp and rob Peter to pay Paul in the church? Just as long as lay people ignore God's ownership of all they are and have. Too many laymen, like that rich, young ruler, go away sorrowfully when confronted with the price of following Christ.

A sermon nowadays which summons the zeal to warn against laying up treasures in heaven, instead of investing on earth, alerts about as much interest as a stamp collectors' convention. As a matter of fact, it raises the proposition among some as to whether or not the minister needs to be psychoanalyzed—what with all that talk about unearthly stuff. What's he talking about? Is he crazy? Regardless of the pagan reactions, still it must be declared that the way one makes his money is as important as how he spends it; that the nine-tenths must be handled with a devoted sense of values, as well as the one-tenth.

But it is right at the point of America's sense of values that she needs to take stock. Think of it: in a world in which millions have never experienced the sensation of a filled stomach, our nation spends multimillions to prevent gaining too much weight. We spend more for chewing gum than we do for educational scholarships; more for greeting cards than for medical research. Last week, a resident of this southern city of a million people and over a thousand churches, left a fortune to five cats! Enough money to relieve the heartache of hundreds of poor families—left to five house cats. How pagan can human nature become? What distorted sense of values calls the plays today!

The truth would be fragmented if I did not sound the note that there is a day of accounting ahead for us all. God is the surest of collectors. And though we have the freedom to ignore His teachings about how to handle things, we do not have the freedom from the penalties of willful ignoring. A day when a trial balance is run on the ledgers of life and God draws a red line under every personal account is fixed on the calendar of eternity. This is not a threat; it is certain fact. What sort of story will the work sheet tell? Will the

153

entries show more spent for the stomach than the mind? More for pleasure than happiness? More for things than people?

Harvey Cushing wrote the biography of Sir William Osler in such an intriguing way that one can see the noble man come alive in the pages. Osler's two passions were medicine and religion. About the latter Cushing wrote, "You can tell the greatness of the man by the kind of entries on his check stubs." Flipping back one year through the cancelled stubs of his financial transactions would produce a ton of guilt in the mind of the average Christian.

Tolstoi brings this moment of truth into clear, sharp focus. His greedy character rising at sunup, stands before the black earth, ready to run his race. The terms of the race: all the land he could run over from a given stake driven in the ground to which he could return by sunset would be his for 1,000 rubles. Bright and early he was there. He ran over many acres, thrilling at the thought of his new-found wealth, thrilling to the feel of deep, black topsoil packing beneath his swift feet. At high noon the avaricious racer turned back so as to make valid his claim by trying to reach the stake before the setting of sun. Summoning all the strength left in his tired legs, he came within a few yards of the stake, and fell dead! The judges took a shovel and stepped off six feet of all that ground he had run across, dug a grave and placed him in it. Six feet! That's all he really needed. In the final lap of life, that is all any man needs. Let's face it and live accordingly.

Too few Christians are in trouble because of insistence that religion should be applied to economics as well as to doxologies.

Domestic Trouble

That time-honored bastion, the home, is losing its honor. It is fast becoming a substation where members of the family wait before the glass-eyed monster of television while another is using the automobile. Instead of being a refuge from the storms of business competition, social frustration and noisy strife, too often the home adds to the tension. Now, when religion demands that a home be peaceful and happy, that the members of the family live in love and harmony, and the demands cause trouble, what course of action should be taken? Is religion to be silenced in the interest of synthetic peace? Not at all. Until more of this type of trouble occurs, pagan inclinations in many homes will continue to grow until every vestige of decency is lost. A recent survey showed that 58 per cent of all the members represented in one of the major Protestant denominations serve liquor in their homes. It does not take an Isaiah to predict the future calibre of the children and their offspring, because such neo-sophistication fails to admit that along with this damaging menu usually are found allied components: lack of constructive companions, failure to participate in spiritual matters, and acquiescence to sordid mediocrity.

Yes, Jesus intrudes in the close-knit fraternity of a family, dividing by His sword of truth one member from another when the division means new direction for one or both. Remember His own family? Even near the end of His earthly ministry, they did not understand either His purpose or His spirit. They came down to Jerusalem to take Him back to Nazareth, believing Him to be beside Himself. God had rather see one child a Christian in a big family with its attendant tension, than the most placid peace among them all without one being saved.

Now, it is true that religion often has been the wedge between some members of a family unnecessarily. In such cases there has been too much talk about religion and too little evidence of its validity shown in action. But this is no reason to cease all talk about the subject. It is the better part of wisdom to face up to the issues, deal with the facts, then let truth have time to ripen, influence, and win.

"Darling, if you will just give up that everlasting running to church, I'll buy you anything you want and we would have peace in our family." These disturbing words had been said many times before, but Mary Ann paid them no attention. "That is just it, John," she answered him, "money can't buy the thing I want most—it isn't for sale. It is free by God's grace and I would never surrender it for your sake nor for the sake of what you call peace in our home." So, she continues to come to church without him. He never loses an opportunity to jeer with sadistic sarcasm at her religion. She

155

knows what it means to be in trouble, in her home, because of her religion. God must reserve a special portion of divine compensation for that kind of discipleship.

Social Scene—Racial Strife

Trouble? Indeed one can find it here if nowhere else. The last decade has witnessed the crumbling of old empires along with disintegration of alliances and political arrangements. Millions are marching from appalling servitude to an unknown future. But they are marching nonetheless. Today the church stands at the crossroads of decisive action; the direction taken can determine the ultimate destiny of civilization. The oppressed and downtrodden are making a decisive bid for their place under the sun. To ignore this march of men is to forfeit our right in the struggle that decency, fairness, honesty and equality might win.

A conspiracy of silence has quieted many voices which should have been heard on this rife issue. Instead of leading the people through a morass of wilderness-like, hazy thinking, the leaders often have been led. "We do not well: this day is a day of good tidings, and we hold our peace." This line from the Syrian lepers of the Old Testament is an honest confession for modern prophets whose muteness is as pronounced as the one about whom it was said that he could be silent in seven languages. It does look as though we could be vocal in at least one language.

What has the church to say about the tension which tightens every day among various races? What reasons compel a prophetic voice? The fact that some politicians have used the issue to traffic in human life is reason enough. Often this traffic has provided an effective smoke screen behind which a politician covered his own lack of qualifications for office. Human life is not a pawn for political chess players, nor is it a football to be kicked around by toes of sectional expediences. Every defensive mechanism employed by those who would perpetuate the myth of racial superiority has compounded what already was a gigantic problem. Many of the very people who should have helped solve this problem became part of the problem itself. There is far more heat than light on the racial issue, and where a noxious, emotional miasma exists, one fires from the hip in all directions. Where reaction to the question at hand is deep-seated to the point of being reflexive, there is more inflammation than inspiration. All the talk about social betterment and racial harmony is little more than empty semantics unless genuine integrity motivates those who do the talking. So long as sectional axes are to be ground, or provincial expediences call the plays, or political ambitions advanced, then so long will this problem curse the human race's bid for decent living.

There are those who insist that Christian religion has nothing to say about man's relation to his fellow man—especially, if one be of another color. Preach the gospel, they contend, and leave the race issue to the legislators. That is our trouble now. It has been left to courts and caucuses and the end result is confusion, contradiction and increased animosity. Silence is no defense against evil. "Freedom is placed in jeopardy more by those who refuse to exercise it than by those who will not permit it." There is no safety to be found in the dark. There are times when silence is golden, and there are times when silence is yellow. It is high time the church found out which is which.

Christ's message was a forthright facing of all that appears in the human equation, bringing to bear the relevance of God's truth without fear, indecision or consequence. Take what Jesus had to say about man's personal relationships with other men out of the New Testament and what is left? Courage ever is in close proximity to a cross.

It is a certainty that this is no time to dwell in ivory towers of idealism, dreaming of utopias, extolling the virtues of ethical presuppositions, and never facing the ugly facts of realism. There are feelings of unity and understanding which exist only in the imaginations of many without commensurate effort to translate the imaginary into practical reality. The idealism of eternity must be brought to bear on the realism of time. Contact must be made if man, as he is, shall ever be as he ought to become in God's sight. There is no place along the firing line where immunity is assured those who would volunteer to fire. Nor is this a time when leaders are to sur-

157

render their right to lead through unnecessary parading of their own unique visions. A train engine, disconnected from freight cars, is not pulling the load, but merely demonstrating its own speed. Christian idealism is not compensatory fiction—it is relevant redemption.

The resurgence of racial tension should be viewed in the light of historical perspective. 1961 can best be understood in the light of 1861 and 61 A.D. Any student of anthropology and sociology knows that the blight of mobs, hysteria, blind prejudice runs in cycles and is as old as the human race. The Egyptians segregated the Israelites, pressing them into meniality and agonizing servitude. Greeks, in the zenith of their culture, regarded others as barbarians. Subsequently, Romans looked upon the Syrians as fit for nothing more than vassal property. The Chinese voiced their walled-in exclusiveness by calling all outsiders "foreign devils." India's caste system exists despite all the piety of her million holy men. Even the monotheism of Palestinian Jews did not rid them of the religious notion that they were God's chosen ones. Regarding Samaritans as half-breeds, they refused even to walk through the Samaritan country. The Jews were chosen for service, not for salvation, by merit. Today, the same sin, in bigger dimensions, divides that troubled country of Palestine as Jew faces Arab in racial belligerance. What a heritage of bigotry, blindness, and hatred! From these centuries of accumulated estrangement, modern man finds plenty of encouragement in his efforts to partition God's world into preferential spheres where some enjoy the best at the expense of all the others. This is an ignominious activity which God cannot bless.

Now and then a voice is raised proposing that all the Negroes in America be sent to their native land. (Usually, the proposal has about as much merit as the proposer has knowledge of history or geography.) Where is a Negro's native land? If the proposal were taken seriously, and Americans followed consistent logic, then all white men would have to be deported to England, Europe or elsewhere. These American acres were hardly the native land of its present Caucasian inhabitants. The ugly fact is that not one Negro asked to be brought to the new world. Instead, he was forcibly

158

transported by scheming white men. The Duke of York, through his connections with the "wild new country" bargained with Yankee buccaneers to provide a pool of manual laborers for the river-boats, factory hands and kitchens of the wealthy. To unload the booty from the Far East required big muscles and the black man was so equipped. But the extreme winters of the North and East proved too much for the man from Equatorial Africa. Then a bargain was struck with Southern plantation owners to employ the slaves in the fields of rice, indigo and cotton. Once again the economic interpretation of history is brought to light, as an objective historian knows quite well. Under the hot sun of the South the Negro felt at home, learned to love parts of it, and loves it to this very day. But the prospering Southerner became a source of envy and, later, of contempt. Only then did the rank and file of Easterners become emotionally involved in the issue of slavery. The point is that slavery was morally wrong from the beginning, but the hue and cry of indignation was strangely mute until after the slave proved economically unprofitable to his original owners.

Time served to compound this predicament and the tragedy of all our national tragedies—the War Between the States—broke out. The ugly scab which tried to cover that wound in which brother fought brother, remains unhealed a hundred years later. Sudden freeing of four million slaves among twelve million whites gave rise to counter-intimidation, domination, carpetbaggers, scalawags, Union soldiers pulling up the last turnip, disenfranchisement, Ku Klux Klans, and fixing of sectional antipathies.

Without knowing these facts one is off base when trying to probe the inner motivation and thinking of many who are involved in racial incidents. While these historical facts in no sense of the word justify racial strife, they help explain much of its expression.

At what place is a child of God to relate himself to the battle for human right? Who has the right answer? Radicals? Conservatives? Moderates? Obviously, the solution is not in law or ethical presuppositions; these will not lessen the tension, though law is necessary to regulate man's external rights and privileges. Ultimately, law is not the basic solution. Prohibition taught us that just to

159

pass a law did not stop men from drinking. If social progress is measured solely in legal equations, grace and love will never play the field.

The answer lies in the old, old truth, neglected too long: peace and harmonious relations will come between all races when each member becomes a reconciler in the spirit of Jesus Christ. And not until! The prevailing disenchantment calls for full commitment to God, knowing that He must be God of all or He will not be God at all. The answer lies not in compulsion but in conversion; reconciliation means nothing without repentance and redemption. Physical closeness is meaningless without psychological nearness. It is too much to expect changed living from unchanged lives. So, we must start at the beginning—in man's heart—if we are to progress toward the destiny of decency under God.

THE ULTIMATE QUESTION: THEN WHY AREN'T YOU IN TROUBLE BECAUSE OF YOUR RELIGION?

If the foregoing contentions have Scriptural validity, then why aren't you in trouble because of your religion? Sin's grip hasn't loosened, evil still assaults the bastions of God with unrelenting ferocity, Herod still seeks the Nazarene to dispose of Him, Annas and Caiphas are reincarnated in many forms today, jealous of any pure movement which would sweep through their foul souls to purge and cleanse. If truth still hurts, and sin is still sin, then why do we fare so well seeing that our forebears in the faith were burned at the stake, fed to arena lions or rotted in dungeons? Indeed, why? Is it that we have feared similar consequences to the point that our courage has wilted to cowardice, our faith has been shorn of its daring and our love atrophied to lust and sentiment?

Religion for us is too respectable. With one arm around Christ and the other around Caesar, today's prophet insists that he can be a regular fellow, intimate with both Christ and Caesar, without any semblance of contradiction or shame. What the church needs is more enemies! Then we could have legitimate targets, instead of firing indiscriminately at one another. Trouble because of religious

160

involvement, trouble as the rightful consequence of living under the mandate of a cross, trouble issuing from refusal to be mixed into a world of paganism, which would mean losing all spiritual identity or individuality—this is what Jesus promised. But He also promised that through adversity He would be present to sustain and direct.

"But Bishop, you must come down and see for yourself. This pastorate is one battleground after another," a young minister wrote. After receiving several such letters of bitter anguish, the bishop visited the little community where the young theologian was desperately floundering. "Nothing I do seems to please them; why, these folks are crucifying me," he lamented. After listening for an hour or two to his verbal desperation, the bishop said, "My young friend, you say these people are crucifying you, and that I just must get you another church to serve or you can't stand it. Well, there is one difference between you and your Saviour; He did not come down from His cross!"

Thorn in the Flesh

8

The Greatest Affliction is never to be afflicted.

Until life's steel is tempered, cowards pass for heroes.

I will not cant . . .
Nor say that grief's slow wisdom makes amends
For broken hearts and desolated years.[1]

His LIFE WAS a storm of paradoxes. A strange mixture of courage and timidity, of strength to the point of boasting, of weakness to the point of arousing pity, yet, in the annals of the human race, few have seized life with firmer grip or given to it more intelligent meaning than Paul of Tarsus. In Christendom's annals, few, if any, have equaled the performance in problematic living of this singular, determined man whose life was a walking civil war. Proud, brilliant, fanatically zealous for any cause he supported, sometimes impulsive, often negative to the point of asceticism, but always willing to relate mind and mood to God's higher purposes, his change of name from Saul to Paul was no more revolutionary than his change of attitude and disposition.

In man's painful climb to a higher plateau of sensible living, it must be admitted that God's human creation is not perfected—that man moves on through modifications, mutations, adaptations, trying to relate his eternity-stamped soul with his time-printed flesh. Since his gifts are in earthen vessels, the flesh is ever a concern. The nature of man's vessel admits disease, accident, hurt and death. To ignore the reality of these limitations is to run headlong into cynicism, despair and futility. The problems of a good God and an evil world, why the innocent suffer, why cancer could be a part of God's creation, why evil men call the plays for righteous men with

[1] Edward Robert Bulwer Lytton, "The Wanderer In Italy. A Love-Letter," 29.

162

inevitable injustices and inequities—these problems and a legion of similar ones must be given some sort of honest answer if the human race is to have any semblance of significance or right to interpret God as more than a tyrant or cruel sadist. A worthy conception of God must grow out of the right answers to some of the foregoing questions. Recite all the catechisms in existence, genuflect before every kind of altar, attend church with unbroken consistency, pay tithes, visit the sick—all these will yield but scrawny, spiritual dividends until a person comes into a lofty, noble conception of God and what God does and refuses to do in human life.

Listen to Paul's story—it contains explosive components of regeneration and rejection. He could have given it either direction. Fortunately, for himself and for us, he took a minus sign, crossed it by a vertical commitment which made of the minus sign a wondrous plus. Where the two lines bisected, they formed a cross. On its beams this man of Tarsus nailed his own ego, surrendered his arrogant ambitions, and bore his hard lot with manly dignity, converting a stumbling block into a steppingstone. His was a magnificent romance in struggle, a work of art in flesh and blood, a human being tortured into genius. And it all happened because of a thorn in his flesh! What at first looked like a stroke of divine negligence in creation became a mystifying, confounding, aggravating divine irritant, without which Paul probably would have been just another "good" man. But the thorn was there and a close scrutiny of it can mean the difference in the reader's life—the difference between being good on one hand and being good for something of divine pleasure on the other.

Let this man speak of his own account:

Lest I should be exalted above measure through the abundance of the revelations, there was given to me a *thorn in the flesh*, the messenger of Satan to buffet me, lest I should be exalted above measure. For this thing I besought the Lord thrice, that it might depart from me. And He said unto me, My Grace is sufficient for thee; for my strength is made perfect in weakness. Most gladly therefore will I rather glory in my infirmities, that the power of Christ may rest upon me. Therefore I take pleasure in infirmities, in reproaches, in necessities, in persecutions, in distresses for Christ's sake; for when I am weak, then am I strong. *II Corinthians 12:7–10.*

Some present-day psychologists would dismiss these words as being the typical babblings of a neurotic, who had found in religion an escape hatch where easy rationalizing led to the daily confirming of his fanaticism. But let us go slowly. Dismissing the account so easily may mark us as the neurotic rather than Paul! His record still stands without equal: a record of triumphs where weaker men would have buckled under and given up a hundred times, but where Paul did not give up at all.

FACT AND NATURE OF HIS THORN

His was no functional ulcer, no minor aggravation conjured up by self-pity or imagination. Here was no badge of a "successful businessman" merely chronicling for history a sour, malfunctioning disposition. It would be both unfair and untrue to conclude that Paul's thorn was merely a minor irritant exaggerated by a hectic itinerary or devout admirers who wrote the record for him. Neither is the case. Rather, his thorn was a daily drain on body and nerves, a continual process. Good evidence leads us to believe that it was more than an occasional annoyance. Instead, it was a painful presence, crippling to his enjoyment, and frustrating at times to his full efficiency. In some of the things said, he implied that it was humiliating, awakening in some folks a sort of pity which is mingled with contempt. It was decidedly real!

The guesses as to the nature of this thorn are almost as varied as human diseases. Among the advantages of not being able definitely to identify its nature is the fact that throngs of devout, suffering Christians have drawn inspiration from Paul's handling of his thorn, who would not have been able to do so had its nature been known. For instance, if his weakness was weak eyes, as one theory contends, basing it on Paul's words, "See what large letters . . ." then primarily those who suffer from similar maladies would be inspired by his victory.

Many theologians believe Paul suffered recurrent attacks of malaria. Many of the low, swampy lands in which he lived and worked were mosquito infested. Malaria was common and ofttimes fatal.

A larger group of interpreters believe Paul's thorn was a combination of psychosomatic factors involving mind and body. Perhaps it was chronic worry which produced maddening cycles of elation and despair. A nature which burned with incandescent brilliance is a good candidate for these extremes. Or, perhaps the hounding Judaizers who dogged his steps wherever he went ever reminded him that his so-called success with the Gentiles did not nullify his failure with his own people. Perhaps an acute memory of his equally dedicated zeal to persecute Christians before his conversion kept cropping out in low moments when energies were waning. In unguarded moments did he permit that sanguine drama to be played back before his eyes? The stoning of Stephen, the dying agony of anonymous followers of the Nazarene, dashed hopes of bright-eyed youth who preferred death of immortality to existence in time without conscience or courage—could these have been part and parcel of memory's anatomy?

Still others believe an inferiority complex nagged at Paul throughout his public life. As supposed basis for this belief, they cite the passages in which boasting and self-justification seem to predominate. Such compensative mechanisms are usual procedures in such a personality. But little credence can be given this belief since his total words must be considered, and the context in which he spoke them.

Was his thorn an emotional imbalance which he could not resolve, whether it expressed itself in a hounding necessity of duty, or a restive compulsion to be up and on the way with an inordinate concern for young churches whose leadership left much to be desired? At any rate, the nature of the thorn is not the chiefest concern. What Paul did about it is the central issue.

INTEGRITY OF ATTITUDE IMPERATIVE

Let us not put words in Paul's mouth. If we are to understand the evolution of his own interpretation, then we must walk, step by step, with him through his travail, struggle and despair. Reaching the top of the mountain by seeing a divine purpose in his thorn was not easy for him, any more than it is easy to ascend a mountain by casually strolling.

An honest attitude toward any of life's experiences is the first requirement of understanding. This man of God had no morbid sentimentality about the thorn: he saw in it an evil thing. As a matter of fact, he called it a "messenger of Satan." But what did Satan have to do with it? Is he God's delivery boy? All the way back to Job, men have put forth clumsy efforts to answer this question. No answers place the final period at the end of a satisfying conclusion. Suffice it, for the purpose at hand, that if Satan was the agent of delivery, still God was the source of its origin. Quite naturally Paul, being a Jew, would attribute all good things to God and all evil things to Satan. The Hebrew people placed every benefit within the province of God. Conversely, they credited every negative occurrence to the account of evil. A Christian runs no risks of misrepresenting God when contending that Satan could deliver nothing to human hands without God's permission. I am glad Paul called it by its rightful name: an evil thing. He was no neurotic enjoying bad health, no ascetic reeking with self-righteous piety whose halo showed through self-imposed martyrdom. An evil thing he called it in that it was sent "to buffet me." "To beat me around" is a more understandable expression.

Here is a good juncture to raise a warning: the ease of saying "the devil did this to me" is too pronounced. Many times neither the devil nor God had anything at all to do with some of the predicaments in which we suffer. Many, if not most, of the adverse experiences of life are explained by intemperance, unpaid debts, improper sleep and dieting, internal hypertensions triggered by unforgiveness, hate or miserliness, and the logical harvest of intentional and known sowings. Better be honest to admit that these are the facts, rather than gloss over them by imputing some mysterious, otherworldly interpretation.

If a person views his maladies apart from divine providence, that person is miserable to the grave. Somewhere, somehow, purpose—God's purpose—must be considered in every human thorn which is

166

not of the individual's accounting. Is there a divine purpose in the thorn? This is the question we want to answer. If there is not such a purpose, then remove by any type of surgery the painful, festering intruder! Otherwise, man is foolish to grope along with no satisfying conviction as to why or for whom! When desperation's surgery cannot remove a thorn whose presence makes no human or divine sense, then other paths are open to the sufferer. But, I warn, none of these paths leads to light. The dubious therapy of saying that the thorn is not really there, or that it isn't a thorn, or it all depends on how one looks at it—such pale deception represents the silliest and least effective handling of the thorn. It is pain enough to be pricked, let alone adding to the pain an additional and unnecessary penalty of mental confusion. Much that parades in the name of Christian faith is little more than witchcraft and cruel superstition. Shrines over the world reputedly claiming cures where medicine could not help, itinerant "healers" who pack into the claims of faith things that faith doesn't even claim for itself—these grew primarily from the magnitude of human suffering and tragic desperation to relieve that suffering. No, it is not good enough to contend that if one had more faith, or could think positively, or convince himself that things are not as they seem, all his troubles would disappear. Cancers are malignant cells, and all soothsayers combined do not change that bio-chemical fact! Thorns can pierce sensitive flesh and the subsequent pain is as real as the flesh it penetrates.

"I BESOUGHT GOD THREE TIMES"

When a man is thorn-infested, the proper court of appeal is the Great Physician. There is no waiting period, no crowd blocks the entrance to the soul clinic called prayer. God was no stranger to Paul. Being thoroughly trained in Rabbinical literature, he knew about God's omniscience, and his conversion to Christianity taught him about God's caring love. So, if God knew all about him and cared as well, what course of action would be more justified and consequential than beseeching God, soliciting God's help in removing the thorn? All the abuses of prayer notwithstanding, it still is valid procedure. The Father-son relationship means that there is access to the Father at any time. No appointment is needed.

But why ask God for anything if He already knows about our needs and has promised to meet them? If honest, searching faith asks this question, then it deserves one type of answer. But if muted lips which have been silenced by distrust and cynicism ask it, it should receive a different answer. Why ask? Petition is but one kind of praying, a kind justified only when in the context of a nobler petition, "Thy will be done." All praying isn't a "give me" monologue. Some spend hours in intercession for others and in adoration of God, exalting Him while forgetting themselves. In these magnificent moments, petition doesn't enter the picture. Prayer is faith expressed through belief that God both hears and heeds. It is union of soul with divine presence in awesome, yet unapologetic communion. There is value in taking our burdens to the Lord, even if we can't leave them all there. A return trip is happily possible. How could a brief chat once or twice a decade suffice anyway? It will not —for the child of God who knows his Father as redeemer and Lord.

"I besought the Lord three times." If the truth were known, this number would be nearer three thousand and one times. Intensity of aggravation in pain sometimes makes one's whole life an upward inclination of thought and word—an endless prayer where no permission is granted a final Amen.

As inexplicable and mystifying as his thorn was God's refusal to remove it. Paul would not conclude that God was unable to remove it. But why was He unwilling to do so? When prayers are denied, what are we to conclude? That God does not hear? That, though hearing, He does not heed or care? Shall we say that the promise of Jesus, "Ask and ye shall receive," applied only to the first-century Christians and not to the rest? How shall we stem the tide of men and women who go away from God and Christian faith because they feel their prayers have been ignored? Well, there are negative answers which need a thorough debunking. Refuge sought in muteness is no consolation. To stop praying because one did not get his order filled is childish. Pursed lips on faces of many church members, however, speak of this sorry recourse. If we ask and the "dumb stars glitter 'no reply,'" least of all can we regard the effort as waste of time. A silent, but belligerent antagonism toward God is worse than trying to live with the mystery of no answer. Surly sourness, while being human, is hardly being intelligent when it comes to probing the depths of prayer, response and divine reaction.

Mrs. K found herself caught in such a vortex of indecision recently. After she had been ill for months and had suffered through several operations, the members of the Sunday school class she had taught were asked to pray daily for their teacher. But each day her condition seemed to worsen. Finally, bitterness consumed her and she wrote the class, "You know, the more you pray for me to get well, the worse I get." Now: was prayer doing either? Was it making her worse or well?

There are several positive approaches when prayers seem to be denied. For instance, delays may not mean denials. His answer is not an unqualified "no." The fact that the exact fulfillment of the prayer was not forthcoming does not mean an adamant refusal on God's part. Modern man cannot connect God to a stop watch, or a rheostat or an escalator. Our nervous impatience is poor tack for divine favor, anyway. And if a thousand years in His sight are as one day, then this morning's prayer and its expected answer should reckon with this fact.

Time is the factor. Syncopation in music enhances its rhythm. The momentary delay of one note accentuates both it and the following note when sounded. Just so in human experience. Some delay in receiving what we deem valuable merely enhances it, once it appears.

He was the last man left alive on the life raft. Being too sick to plunge into the sea from fear and desperation as others had done, the man drifted for days in the broiling sun of the Pacific. He cursed God for allowing the ship to sink in the first place. Then he profaned God for sending no rain for his parched throat. A few days later, however, the raft washed ashore on a pleasant, fruit laden island where the tired, cynical, sickly man was nursed back to health. Little did he know that during his long days at sea, as painful as they were, God was using the hot sun and salty breeze to cure him of tuberculosis. Were his prayers answered? No, not in the way he had asked. But in a way more far-reaching than the man had imagined, yes, his prayers were answered.

Part of the process in valid praying is watching. When a human soul posts its guard, attacks by intruders are repelled, and illuminating sights are recorded in the mind. Watching the way God does things is wholesome gymnastics for our world-inured minds. God can grant the substance of the prayer without the form in which we ask.

If we were to receive all our desires from God, it might mean the ultimate impoverishment of our souls. God could not be a party to such a curse. The Bible still records this singular commentary: "He [God] gave them their request; but sent leanness into their soul." What was desired may often have proved fatal, in the light of eternity.

Saint Teresa in one of her challenging phrases, marked by the quaintness of her consecration wrote in her Journal: "Lord, when wilt Thou cease to strew our path with obstacles?" And the Lord spoke to her in answer: "Murmur not, for it is thus that I treat My friends." At which Teresa sighed and said: "Ah, dear Lord, and that is why Thou hast so few."[2]

One thing is historically clear to a casual observer: God never demonstrates His loving care for His children more than when He ignores some of our requests. In *Antony and Cleopatra*, Shakespeare has Menecrates say,

> We, ignorant of ourselves,
> Beg often our own harms, which the wise powers
> Deny us for our good; so find we profit
> By losing of our prayers.[3]

There are times in the lives of mature Christians when prayer is progressive agony. When God arrests the shallow disposition of man by any providential method, the pause can become a curriculum in which one's sense of awe and undoing expand. Such ex-

[2] Quoted in *The Speaker's Bible*. Edited by Edward Hastings, Aberdeen, Scotland, 1933, p. 198.
[3] Act II, Sc. 1.

170

pansion is the rightful dimension for God's future dealings. But the direst expansion, the most intense rigors of God's chastening initiative, do not remotely approach the progressive agony in Gethsemane.

It is no compliment that each Christian has to learn this difficult truth not once but many times. Some facets of divine truth could be accepted by the regimen of trust and faith without having to experience the negative curriculum. St. Monica prayed in a seaside chapel on the African coast that God would prevent her son, Augustine, from going to Rome. Fearing what a big city might do to an impressionable young man, she implored God to do anything to prevent his going. Even as she prayed with agony and petition, her son sailed for Italy. But in the licentious, pagan city, her son met Ambrose who led him to the light, and Augustine became a devout Christian. Just suppose God had literally answered Monica's prayer back in Africa. If the thing for which we plead and the way we choose for it to be granted be oft denied, it is because God has something greater, better, in mind than our finite, limited prayers can foresee.

Adoniram Judson prayed hours at a time for his wife's health. He buried her nonetheless—and two children. Then he prayed to God for release from prison in order that he might carry on his work as a Christian missionary. Instead of release, mosquitoes swarmed in and punctured his naked feet which were strapped upward, until they swelled to twice their normal size. Some answer from God! But: God chose a different way and time than Judson had chosen. While being denied exact things, conditions and time, the values inherent in those conditions were graciously granted . . . and more. Today an Eastern nation stands as glowing testimony to the value of Judson's life. The deep thrusts of his soul were being accomplished not in his way but beyond his way, in God's.

THE FUTILITY OF INTERCESSORY PRAYER WHEN ONE'S THORN IS DIVINELY IMPLANTED

Can a person alter God's plan for an individual's life by sentiment and supplication? Will constant pulling on God's heartstrings modify His intention? Recorded religious lore contains poor answers to these questions.

God did not remove Paul's thorn, regardless of how many times He was asked to do so. And for His own excellent reason. God did not place the thorn merely as a challenge for Paul to ask that it be removed. No such theatrics characterize the Creator! Had Paul known in advance that God wasn't going to pull out the irritant, then he would not have fought, asked, doubted, chafed, rebelled and eventually resigned himself to its presence. Through each of these processes Paul hammered out the steel of a stalwart soul. Thus was the presence and purpose of the thorn justified.

There is a type of resistance in Christian discipleship which can be ruinous. If Paul could not kick against the pricks, neither can we. Resisting God's holy designs is futile effort. Man is no match for his Maker. Jacob's wrestling with an angel seemed absurd enough, but human will pitted against divine omnipotence is inconceivable. The truth is that God is going to accomplish certain things with or without our consent. No personal freedom of choice is violated at such times, since God can do with His own what He likes. He can veto and override man's negative vote in order to rule in sovereignty and love. This is a phase of truth that seldom is heard in our midst. Too much is made of the individual's free choice. Man's freedom ends at the point where God's pleasure demands the right of way. He will get the appointed task out of us one way or the other: either by the ministries of love, primroses and sunsets, or by the bloody whip and maddening dreams.

This sobering conclusion gives no leverage to the old myth that God predestines our lot in life. A thousand dangers are inherent in believing the wrong type of predestination. To say that God has foredetermined how one shall act and react, the mode of life and death, is to conclude that living is no more than fitting into a shallow drama, the purpose of which is known only to God. Man under such conditions would be a puppet drawn by strings. God in such a role would be a dictator denying man freedom of choice. This was the basis for Christendom's pagan reasoning for several centuries in agreeing that if God wanted the heathen saved, He would save him. In Baptist churches, as well as many other denominations, this very day there are people who still hold to the same ignorant belief.

In a very definite way God is related to our past, present and future. But His relationship is one of voluntary guidance instead of rude intrusion. When invited, God enters to transform and direct a person's life. When ignored, however, God will permit the same person to bring his life to a tragic end. If a man drinks himself into a drunken stupor, gets in his car and drives it a hundred miles an hour, plunges over an embankment and kills himself, will anyone conclude that this was his way to die? Man needs no better seedbed for fatalism than the old yet recurring dogma, "what is going to be is going to be," regardless of man's thoughts or deeds. A junior boy or girl can know the answer to this dilemma. Predestination is one of the fine doctrines of the Christian Church and means that God foreknows man's total life, man's responses and manner of his death. But His foreknowledge does not mean His foreactivity; because God knows how a thing will occur does not mean that He determines that it will so occur. Divine will is best thought of as two circles: one within the other. The smaller circle is the area of God's permissive will. Therein all types of evil incidents are mixed with good fortune. Since man is free even to curse God, this freedom is exercised within the sphere of the Lord's permissive will. But the smaller circle exists within the circumference of the larger circle: God's intentional will. All that He permits is not intended. But to rupture the two would violate man's wondrous privilege to say yes or no for himself.

Such is the reasoning which caused Paul to say that the thorn "was given to me." He did not say that it was thrust on him, or crudely forced upon him, but the word employed suggests a loving will behind it. The same word is used to tell of the cup which Jesus drank. The cup's content was prepared by hands of hate, but God handed it to Him. The distinction makes all the difference in understanding such ineffable mystery.

WHEN GOD'S GRACE IS SUFFICIENT

God did not answer Paul's prayer but He answered Paul. The content of the answer exceeded anything that the apostle imagined. My, how easy it would have been for God to have breathed one healing breath through this single Jew and cured him of all maladies—thorn included. But to what avail would perfect health have been? Instead of a quick summary answer, God revealed Himself in a wonderful statement: "My grace is sufficient for you." Here is one truth that cannot be comprehended academically. It must be experienced. When the prospects of relief are slim or dim, man is in a good position to apply for God's grace. Few men ever acknowledge their utter need for God at any other time. Yes, there is danger in short-term results, but faith takes a chance every time. This discipline called faith is "patience with a lamp in it."

God's grace so confounds human efforts to comprehend it that it leaves us with poor inclination even to try. Most times grace is assigned to the arena of abstract virtues which sound good by pronunciation but which mean little more than words. Browning touched on the nature of God's grace:

> God, for our own good, makes the need extreme,
> Till at the last He puts forth might and saves.[4]

Divine grace is a compensatory virtue. When one loses one of the five senses, the sense of hearing, for instance, all remaining senses are accentuated in a type of compensation for the loss of this one. God never subtracts without either adding or multiplying. This is the nature of His grace. There are two ways of helping a man with a load on his back: either to take off the load or to strengthen his back. God often chooses to do the latter.

"Hey, Mister, can you spare me a dime for a cup of coffee?" a dirty, haggard man asked another who slowly passed by. As the well-dressed, middle-aged man reached in his pocket for a coin, he looked into the eyes of the beggar. He noticed a familiar expres-

[4] Robert Browning, "The Ring and the Book."

sion, a face that remotely resembled one he had known somewhere previously. "Do I know you?" he asked the impassive beggar. Before an answer could be given, his identity came clearly to mind. "Frank, what on earth has happened to you? We were fraternity brothers fifteen years ago. You were prospering in your own business the last time I heard of you. Will I give you a dime for a cup of coffee? Of course, and whatever else you need!" Reaching in his coat pocket, he pulled out a checkbook, wrote out a check and thrust it in the hand of his former college pal. "Go buy yourself a suit of clothes, new shoes, get a haircut and shave and start all over, Frank." The shocked beggar looked down at the check, then up in the eyes of his friend and thanked him. But as the beggar approached the bank to cash the check, he noticed many well-dressed people in the newly appointed lobby. He looked at the tellers with their efficient, polished manners and turned back to the front door without cashing the check.

The next day the same two men met again, and the beggar's appearance was unchanged. "Why didn't you buy the new clothes? Why didn't you clean yourself up as I asked you? What did you do with the money?" Pulling out the uncashed check, Frank showed it to his donor and said, "I went down to that fancy looking bank, saw all those well-dressed people, and decided that they would not cash this check anyway, knowing that a bum like myself had either forged it or stolen it." Whereupon his friend rebuked him: "Listen, Frank, the thing that makes that check good is not your appearance but my signature on it! Go cash it and use it. My name on it is all that is needed."

The same applies to the grace of God for human need. Our merit, be it little or much, is not the issue. Every promise of Almighty God is countersigned by Jesus Christ! The least we can do is to trust Him for His grace.

"STRENGTH IS PERFECTED IN WEAKNESS"

The personal nature of Paul the Apostle explains part of the thorn's necessity. He admitted one of its uses was a safeguard against pride and arrogance. His having been chosen by God for a unique role in Christendom was no reason for self-exaltation. Having been granted the unearthly experience of seeing into the third heaven was basis enough for potential pride. He wasn't lacking in self-confidence from the beginning—a fact of great worth but one which must be re-evaluated day by day.

Two kinds of pride beset humanity: pride of possession, which speaks of elementals, and pride of spiritual achievement. But pride of spiritual achievement, of kingdom accomplishments, is twice as bad as pride of possession, since spiritual pride feeds on the very strength which should produce humility. Honest self-esteem is a healthy virtue; inordinate concern with self's spiritual progress is rank arrogance in God's eyes.

So God had to enroll Paul in the thorn-infested curriculum of adversity in order to graduate him *summa cum laude* in the university of discipleship. As a ship requires stabilizers to prevent its roll and pitch in a heavy sea, as weights on a horse's hooves give steady rhythm to its pace, as shock absorbers cushion the journeyer's ride, as springs in a door's hinge prevent sagging—so a thorn placed in Paul's flesh gave him the stabilizing, even-keeled bearing which was needed before the courts of kings, despots, tyrants and evil men. We would place the same thorn in ourselves were we God and knew what He knows!

The point of Paul's weakness became the place of God's power. How else can God lay bare the human spirit so that the divine spirit can do its work? As long as events and circumstances kept an even tempo, Paul was just another man. Calm seas are no test of a ship's prowess. No ocean liner can be launched in a bathtub. When God has big things in mind, He needs space and dimension. Both are provided in human attitude which is broadened and expanded by the pulling power of divine necessity. Without the refining effects of this painful irritant, in all probability Paul would have faded in the dusty archives of discipleship with about as much accomplishment and notoriety as had Thaddaeus.

> We need as much the cross we bear
> As air we breathe, as light we see

> It draws us to Thy side in prayer,
> It binds us to our strength in Thee.[5]

To some it may sound singularly strange to contend that human frailties can be broad avenues of God's constructive traffic. But it is true. History is resplendent with biographies to prove it. Isaiah, Handel, Galileo, Luther, Keller, Bunyan, Daniel, Stephen,—a noble array! And what is it about a sense of struggle that enhances the life of man? The hard acorn of self begins to expand; tiny specks of sympathy grow into larger, emphatic concerns. Identity with the corps of sufferers is a belonging never terminated in value or time. The invisible bond annexing one cross-bearer to another holds with such fixity and force that eventually all links in the chain are connected to the original Cross-bearer.

There is no intrinsic value in pain or adversity *per se*. Actually, for every one who converts a painful thorn into a place of divine pleasure, there must be ten thousand who give it a cursed direction. Just to suffer in itself is not man's blessing, but his curse. No stone should be left unturned in trying to conquer all human diseases. If this were possible, however, man still remains imperfect in his soul's anatomy. His mind will ever provide enough desert wasteland for growing thorns of providential purpose. The struggle to overcome is the only real value. Muscles developed in the process, which otherwise lie dormant, a sense of human inadequacy which leads to prayer and divine dependence, are but few of the dividends of this paradoxical exercise. To one who is God-initiated, the flesh exists in primary purpose to propel the spirit on its journey Godward.

> To man, propose this test—
> Thy body at its best,
> How far can that project thy soul on its lone way?[6]

These words of Robert Browning through his character Rabbi Ben Ezra find poor hearing in our day, a day which insists that the flesh take precedence over all else, at all costs. If weakness probes the

[5] A. L. Waring, *The Speaker's Bible*, Volume II, Corinthians. Edited by Edward Hastings, Aberdeen, Scotland, 1933, p. 197.
[6] Robert Browning, "Rabbi Ben Ezra." Stanza VIII.

depth of the human heart and thereby deepens its channels for God's indwelling, then weakness is assuredly strength being perfected in the process.

This is no field in which spiritual amateurs can experiment, for in this area, rigorous self-denial which foregoes the comfort of indulging natural ambition and chastises every vestige of vanity, must be given right of way. If you ask for courage, then do not be dismayed when Goliaths appear. If one petitions God for love to increase, then let there be no chagrin when God assigns the petitioner to live among the unlovely. If you ask for faith to be increased, then expect mountains to appear—mountains exactly commensurate to the portion of faith. If one asks for the will of God to be done, then there is good likelihood that it will happen. So, we had better tread softly when approaching God. We should move with caution when we ask anything of Him. You see, He is apt to accommodate us, and if He did, many of us would have to do a complete about-face while denouncing our own will and way. Weakness becomes a finishing school for the rare virtues of submission and resignation. Life always is enhanced by a good fight and Paul stayed in the ring, not shadowboxing, but giving direction to every blow. From the quality of his example millions have drawn strength—not from the fact of his weakness, but from the encounter of weakness with divine strength and the quality resulting therefrom. Rightly estimating one's own strength and weakness is part of the secret of becoming strong. But to hallow weakness as being valuable in itself is to ignore Paul's attitude. He did not go around feeling his own pulse, posing as one whom God was heckling or torturing into a spiritual genius. The world will ignore a self-pittier in travail, but no one will admire the latent victory never won—by overcoming weakness, or, when overcoming is impossible, by glorious acceptance of the weakness.

These are part and parcel of grief's slow wisdom—slow, because of excruciating pain or baffling anguish which is as apt to stupefy and dull man's soul and sense as it is to refine them. But if tears become telescopes to bring heaven into sharp focus, if the same furnace which liquifies gold hardens clay, then who shall call

178

these curses? Horace Bushnell countered a solicitous man's pity for him by saying, "I have learned more of experimental religion since my little boy died than in all my life before." Why? Because the times when one's cup seems as bitter as gall, then at least can be remembered the spiked hand that will help you hold it. Only when God washes our eyes with tears can the eyes see clearly enough God's handwriting through the dull, thorny prose of life.

THE DISCIPLINED ART OF RESIGNATION

Now we approach the most momentous decision in the life of Paul, second only to his conversion on the Damascus Road. It was obvious to him now that God was not going to remove the thorn but would leave it there out of a higher consideration than physical or emotional health. One alternative was to acquiesce by admitting that nothing constructive or effective could be done about it anyway, and therefore fan the fires of cynical distrust and learned, functional atheism. To go ahead, marking off days and years, anticipating the time when they all would be behind him. In a word, rebel, reject, and silently vote against purpose, significance and divine pleasure. This road opened before him alluringly. In following it, however, Paul knew full well that he would be doubling the weight of his cross by adding the tonnage of bitterness and despair. This offered no bright hope. The other road was a fine alternative to the first: resignation to the divinely implanted presence and making the most of a bad situation. This he embraced with full abandon, without the slightest reservation. Then his life of cutting tensions, turbulent torments, maddening dreams and hounding fears changed. Not suddenly, but with such complete metamorphosis that the man speaking in the Second Letter to the Corinthian Church doesn't sound at all like the man speaking in earlier years.

Note his steps of growth: his first comment about the thorn was "a messenger of Satan to buffet me." Step number two deleted Satan's role and assumed the form of numbed neutrality. Less bitterness now, less inclination to classify cause and purpose, more will-

179

ingness to trace at least a faint outline of a friendly hand in the adverse situation. In the third step, like a post-graduate student's compared to the step of one in kindergarten, Paul happily testifies, "Most gladly therefore will I glory in my infirmities that the power of Christ may rest upon me . . . I will take pleasure in infirmities. . . ." That is the apex of contrite virtue, the epitome of surrender. Not only going along with God because of necessity, but graciously, gladly keeping step.

The primary need of modern Christians is some analogous experience by which our shallow egoism could be supplanted by deep abiding resignation to His will and way. Unqualified surrender to God will change this old world from its pagan miseries to pleasureful purpose.

This man said nothing more about expulsion after his resignation. The preoccupying aggravation about his thorn merely made it fester more painfully. But when he accepted it and changed his attitude, though the thorn remained embedded, its pain became more tolerable by virtue of his saying, "I have learned, in whatsoever state I am, therewith to be content." One lays hold of such rare truth by no process other than learning. Christian faith does not remove our burdens; it changes their nature so that we can bear them.

"GLORYING IN INFIRMITIES"

The ultimate step in human emancipation from the world is taking pleasure in divine purposes. This itinerant evangelist could enumerate more ill fortune, adverse conditions and tragic happenings than any dozen disciples of the same faith. Yet, he rose above the minus signs by crossing every one of them into a plus mark by qualitative commitments. How can one rejoice in what is painful, embarrassing and besetting? Singing at midnight, if you please? The secret: his was a supremely precious finding which made reproach and persecution seem trivial by comparison. Darkness became an aura of light, jails became tabernacles of devotion and the curses of sinful men became cries of admission that they had no God! No peace transcends that of an accepted sorrow—pleasureful acceptance in the awesome holiness of glorying. If one does not weigh these words, he runs the risk of impiety or sadism. The joy of a holy antagonism can change one-talent, narrow-gauged people into magnanimous, stalwart souls. Rough, crude edges of unsurrendered personalities can be polished by the emery dust of adversity. It was not too much for Paul to bear one thorn when he remembered that his Christ wore a whole crown of thorns for him. The servant was not better than his Master.

In the real measure of life, it is not the things which happen to us that make the difference; it is what we permit circumstances to do to and through us that matters eternally. The same heat that causes a cut flower to wilt, causes a rooted flower to grow. So it is not in the heat but whether or not there are roots! A cold wind of adversity can make one person denounce his Lord while a similar wind can drive another person closer to his Lord. This strange state of trial in which man is introduced to himself, is either steppingstone or stumbling block, depending on attitude and will. If intelligent will power is permitted to play the field, then the right method of handling trouble is to pass through it as the Israelites did the Red Sea. They did not pitch camp in the sea bed. So, the ultimate criterion is not the nature of one's thorn or how irksome its presence, but how much pure, spiritual essence flows from its festation, how much glory accrues as a result of its stubborn residence.

Among the rare beauties of the botanical world is a lily which is native to Southern India. Petals are arranged with such artful symmetry that the dullest eyes are alerted by its rapturous beauty. Because the lily wilted and atrophied in lush, fertile soil and plenteous moisture, it was transplanted to barren, dry acres; there it flourished among cacti, thorns and spikes. Because of this beauteous adaptation amidst so stultifying an environment, the lily was named "Gloriosa." Paul's acceptance of his thorn for God's glory is rarer than the Indian lily.

And Now Tomorrow

9

Be still my soul—the Lord is on thy side.

"Sufficient unto the day is the evil thereof."—Jesus Christ

WHERE DO WE go from here? Obviously, we cannot stand where we are, for life is like riding a bicycle: either you go on or you go off. The prophets speaking about the future are as varied and distracting as their prophecies. Little comfort or guidance is offered in either. On one extreme stand the nuclear alarmists whose idiom sounds like syntax from Frankenstein: carbon annihilation, mega-death, total obliteration. Standing at the other extreme, of similar worthlessness, are many optimists who see the world getting better and better every day in every way. Between these extremes stand screaming evangelists, historians with their "inevitable" concepts of history repeating itself, and a herd of unthinking millions who have elected, as an alternative to the aforementioned, a kind of placid confusion which they dishonestly call normalcy.

Does the child of God in Christ Jesus have nothing better to say about the future than these? Where is that clear, unapologetic declaration that God has not abdicated His throne, nor will He? Have we forgotten that God still can laugh at the heathen's raging, that "The ungodly are not so but are like the chaff which the wind driveth away"? Admittedly, the wind has not yet driven evil and evil men from their lairs of power and influence. But to acquiesce in the belief that things will always be this bad is to ignore God's time-honored truth: "The kingdoms of this world are become the kingdoms of our Lord, and of his Christ; and he shall reign for ever and ever." The kingdoms of *this world* . . . and while we have

182

no calendar or timetable, we have the promise—a promise which is basis enough for belief and trust.

A NECESSARY DUALISM: WALKING BY FAITH AND SIGHT

A Christ-conditioned attitude, while casting an aura of optimism above the unknown tomorrow, should not blind itself to the realism of the present tense. This is an area of truth so easily obscured by those who think that faith does not have its feet on the ground. Discipleship involves the paradox of one foot on earth and the other in heaven, without leaving the impression of imbalance as one walks.

Faith is not content with saying, "Look what the world has come to"; instead, it shouts as an alternative: "Look who has come to the world!" And despite sordid waywardness in easy evidence, believing faith is quick to see the good, the beautiful, and the pure in life. Remembering that good news moves at snail's pace while evil report travels fast as light, nonetheless, faith sets itself to disseminating wholesome, positive affirmations.

CHRISTIAN OPTIMISM DOES NOT REQUIRE ONE TO BE BLIND TO TODAY'S FACTS

Realism which is hurtful, insidious and cunning cannot be imagined away. Nor can that which denies the reality of pain and poverty be called the kind of faith Jesus practiced or taught. We must look straight into the ugly face of stark realism, see it for what it is: pockmarks, the acne of egoism, deep-creased lines of scowling negation which inevitably follow an unsightly life from which God has taken leave; these constitute the profile. Yet, having seen it, a child of God loses no heart because he knows that the profile of man can be changed into a thing of beauty by God's redemptive love.

Moreover, the present miasma of confusion does not obscure the

183

fact that there are many religious pioneers whom cynics and pessimists know nothing about.

In America alone there are upwards of one hundred and twenty million people who belong to some church or synagogue. One hundred and twenty million! All the mixed motives, and minimum understanding about what it means notwithstanding, the fact remains that this is the first time in history anyone has been able to say as much about his generation.

The worst of men are not bereft of some goodness, some flicker of decency. Christian faith majors on the sinner trying to enhance the chance that such a person will come to a clearer realization of his need for God. The fact that the human race refuses to settle for any other conclusion than religion in some form is an enheartening basis for carrying on. Most atheists are like the man who said, "Yes, I am an atheist, thank God." Though conscience be bludgeoned, still in the few, lucid moments the mind faintly probes life's meaning, source, author, destiny. Under the impact of the right influence, the rankest cynic feels an upward tug, even if he never admits it or gives intelligent direction to the tug.

Rather than feeling that the world is going to the dogs, by reading the daily accounts of incest, murder, arson, theft, and endless combinations of erratic behavior, the child of God should read journals which are not for sale on magazine stands: religious monthlies, weekly journals, which report the activities of hundreds of fine young people. These are the youth in total commitment to their God, who set themselves aside for that special type of living called full-time Christian service. Seeing one clean-faced, highbrowed youth take his stand for God is a sight which outshines a regiment that stands for Satan.

OPTIMISM NOT BORN OF CHRISTIAN FAITH IS VAIN DELUSION

Trying to squeeze some constructive meaning from the tube of today's reality without the perspective of Christian logic and love is futile effort. Looking at sin through rose-colored glasses is poor endeavor for sin's remission. The cross of Christ was sufferable only because it foresaw the crown of triumph. Take one without the other and you have fragmented grief on one hand and vain delusion on the other.

Optimism thus born is many-faceted: It sees the cup half-filled, not half-empty; Christ-centered optimism knows that

> Behind a frowning providence
> He hides a smiling face.

The eye still sees in the center of a storm; hate is but the reverse of the coin of love; the serpent's fangs are seen in the light of its limited powers of destruction; and the cruelest sinner is a potential saint through Christ Jesus. Optimists insist that it is always too soon to quit. These are the residue of a Christ-conditioned attitude toward God and man.

CHRIST'S URGENT EMPHASES ON THE PRESENT

Respecting no postponement, Jesus stated, "I must work the works of him that sent me, while it is day: the night cometh when no man can work." He made it plain that today we are at the bat of life. The fouls which come from half-hearted effort, the fannings-out which result from distraction, are ever under His scrutiny and condemnation. Hit the ball, run with haste, He shouts to this generation. He condemns "spectatoritis" in the passive multitudes as vehemently as He did in the city of Jerusalem. Distance gained in the past can be lost in the present. The valiant pilgrims who brought the torch of civilization thus far did not hand it to us as a cigarette lighter, but as an illuminator for our darkness, and our world's darkness.

Nations can lie dormant for a long time while the parade of men and movements passes them by. Rip Van Winkle sleeps and snores today. Think of it: masses on the march, old kingdoms crumbling, new orders appearing, old coalitions disintegrating and some people oblivious to it all!

> In the world's broad field of battle,
> In the bivouac of life,
> Be not like dumb, driven cattle!
> Be a hero in the strife![1]

ALL WISHFUL THINKING NOTWITHSTANDING, THIS IS THE ONLY WORLD WE HAVE

Despite theological escape artists who impoverish this life by unduly emphasizing life to come, what is wrong with living superlatively in *this* life? All the ills here can be cured by redemptive love! And if a part of the time spent trying to usher in the miraculous millennium were spent in creating the environment and climate for godly living, things would improve appreciably.

Eternal life is present possession for the twice-born. It does not require a detour through crypt or mausoleum for its beginning. The moment one says "no" to self and Satan, and "yes" to God, that moment eternal life begins. "'Tis heaven below my Redeemer to know."

This type of kingdom subject prefers to light a candle rather than curse the darkness. Every time wind blows it out, he relights it. Faith is that willingness of mind and readiness of fingers to keep on striking matches to light the candles blown out by cynical winds. This is the kind which refuses to join the ranks of fatalists. While he cannot answer all the questions, he knows who can. And though he may take his burdens to the Lord and not leave all of them there, he remembers that he can go back again and again, until the load becomes bearable or the back becomes stronger.

MY PERSONAL CREDO

Truth and Right Are Inherently Triumphant—Evil Contains the Seed of Its Own Defeat

The foregoing chapters present, in a loose-knit fashion, something of my own present outlook. Part of these convictions have been

[1] Henry Wadsworth Longfellow, "The Psalm of Life." Stanza 5.

186

hammered out on the anvil of personal experience. That part of them, of course, is more meaningful. I am less inclined to walk into the same fires by which I have been burned before. I am less prone to parrot the cynic's phrase when confronted with the inexplicable; times in which I see no way out, my blindness provides a necessary pause to look up, instead of frantically searching the horizontal. In the heat of battle I never feel alone. Under the power of a divine compulsion, a stronger power from above is strangely present— reassuring, reaffirming the promise that no man will be tempted beyond his ability to resist. My capacity for absorbing the easy rote of "faith's" contentions is shriveling. Some "truths" about God, once accepted in childlike readiness, today are regarded with serious misgivings. This, I say, with no proclivity for self-sufficiency, or the slightest suggestion that mystery has disappeared, or that a hard-headed realism doesn't grant faith its birthright in dimension. But this at least is acknowledged fact rather than pious glossary.

Of this thing I am quite confident: we are not left as strangers standing before a roulette wheel of caprice where our chances for winning are nearly nonexistent. There has been no rigging of life's mechanism. The rigors of doubt and probabilities are ours to wrestle and throw by the muscles of faith's perseverance. While admitting the seas' nauseating turbulence, I do not get the notion that there isn't a Skipper aboard the ship; nor for that matter, that the seas' waves are their own determiner of momentum or direction.

Only now and then does it concern me that God hasn't given man a road map where every turn of the way is underlined in red. Chapter and verse need not be cited for every oral recitation or transliteration. Suffice it that He has given a compass. Going in the general direction will ultimately lead to that specific route number one. Nor is a time table necessary. Strange that anyone would so boldly say this when our lives are guided by clocks, calendars, hours and minutes much as a horse is guided by bits in his mouth; nonetheless, the right evaluation of the hour and minute at hand is employment enough to give balance to the future hours and days. I never had much trouble in directions, anyway, so far as knowing the right road to take when it came to morality, duty and first loyalties. It is as simple as *turning right and going straight*. All the complex shades of relatives should not obscure the absolutes: the regenerate man is to enter that strait gate and keep on walking that narrow pathway. Instead of praying for emergency supplies, I have learned to pray for daily bread.

Then about tomorrow: I know not what the future holds but I know who holds the future. This is the guaranteed basis for going ahead, face up, chin set, eyes forward like one entranced by a radiant, gleaming, though distant scene. The fact that He promises to go with us all the way should be accompaniment enough for total effort on our part. What better company does one need? Who but God could go along—God who knows the way, provides the necessities, charts the course and encourages our steps? "He knows the way, He holds the key, He guides us with unerring hands."

One of the mercies of God is His veiling the future from our eyes. Despite our guesses, prophecies, gambles and predictions, "no man knows what a day brings forth." Nor should he. It is knowing in advance which robs life both of its romance of surprise and its childlike dependence on God, who does know the future. Herein we are admonished to live one day at a time. It speaks of no trust constantly to pry at the lid of the future to get some peep at what it holds. Forcing the petals of a rosebud to open destroys the rose.

Such folly was represented by two British businessmen who fell into the habit of talking shop whenever they were together. In a mood of fanciful imagination, one asked the other, "If you could have anything your heart desires, what would it be?" After pondering the question for a good while, he answered his friend by saying, "If I could have anything, I believe I would ask for a copy of the London *Times* dated ten years ahead." In equally fanciful imagination the man's request was granted. There, with the London newspaper dated a decade in advance, he nervously turned to the stock market quotations. After seeing how certain stocks had risen in value, he threw down the paper and rushed out to make his investments. But as the paper fell on the table, he noticed that the back page contained the obituary column. His name was the first listed among the dead! No, we do not really want to know the future. It is a merciful stroke of God's goodness that we cannot.

This armed confidence is the only valid explanation of those historical daredevils, who for Christ's sake, while facing staggering odds, fought and won. Taking their Nazarene Leader at His word, they became convinced that they were better than the sparrow, or the lilies, or the grass—all of which were divinely fed. Suffused with that inner fire, they faced every type of designed evil, with trembling hands but hearts that were steady.

And we, gazing in that elevated direction of ultimate victory, still must look down and around at the immediate future. Much that is seen is disconcerting. Much of it repels, discourages, thwarts. Yet, the nature of the Way has an uncomfortable nexus with crosses. Expendability is the lot of all who would be obedient servants of their Master. More important than life itself is that Way of life for which millions have bled and died.

THE LONG LOOK

Ah, but it is the quality of that distant profile which should engender fresh confidence and new heart. If one knows that he will win the war, he can fight single battles with more ardor. There is no doubt about ultimate victory. God has made the universe in such a way that righteousness is inherently triumphant while defeat is innate in evil. It looks as though despots and tyrants would learn this fact sooner or later. But each generation must discover and rediscover this fact for itself. The legacy which cannot be handed down is an unswerving belief that good will come out on top in the end. Especially is this true when weak souls exert puny effort against the all-out efforts of dictators.

He speaks best who speaks last, and God has the last word. Hear it: "The kingdoms of this world are become the kingdoms of our Lord, and of his Christ; and he shall reign for ever and ever." That is the fixed certainty of the future! God would not have given the world a matchbox had He not known that the world's framework is fireproof. Discovering this changeless truth, Paul the Apostle left a verbal legacy which is as much a part of his inner

189

soul as the heart was a part of his body: "For I am persuaded, that neither death, nor life, nor angels, nor principalities, nor powers, nor things present, nor things to come, Nor height, nor depth, nor any other creature, shall be able to separate us from the love of God, which is in Christ Jesus our Lord."

New Jerusalem always shows in the background of Armageddon. A victory march, which began at the entrance of a borrowed tomb on a Sunday morning, gained momentum for twenty centuries and shall continue until it reaches the portals where the One who emptied that tomb reigns in victory. There is no place then for whining, simpering self-pity; no quarter for the slow of faith, no time for doubts, no profit in living on probabilities—not when all these wondrous truths are present. Engraved invitations are extended to all who would accept.

Last summer I spent a few days on a Carolina farm. Rain hadn't fallen for several weeks. The vegetation look scalded. Dust and sand cast a pall of gloom over the place. The shallow, backyard well reluctantly gave out its trickle of water as a small pump worked overtime. A lawn sprinkler twirled in lazy, irregular rhythm, hampered by sand in the water. The brown, parched grass welcomed the meager sprinkle with spongelike gratitude.

One afternoon I heard a low rumble, followed by distant echoes. In less than half an hour, thunder was rolling like someone walking on the bass pedals of a mighty pipe organ. A few drops of rain fell. Few, then many, followed by a torrential downpour. In the gratitude of watching rain wrestle the dust, and the symphonic enjoyment which comes while hearing rain on a tin roof, I forgot to turn off the sprinkler. There it kept turning, uncertainly, erratically, as though it were half-embarrassed. I thought: The lawn sprinkler is poor competition for the real thing—the rains from heaven. Yet, until the rains came, the lawn sprinkler's efforts were essential to the life of the grass. Just so with our human, paltry efforts here and now. Though meager and spurty, the human sprinklers must keep on turning. Then, one of these days there will be a deluge of divine initiative, a torrential downpour, when God invades history. We can turn off our little sporadic sprinklers then!

190